IN THE GLORY OF GOD:
MEDIEVAL ART

Titles in the series include:

A Life for God: The Medieval Monastery

Lords, Ladies, Peasants, and Knights: Class in the Middle Ages

Miracles, Saints, and Superstition: The Medieval Mind

The Unholy Crusade: The Ransacking of Medieval Constantinople

IN THE GLORY OF GOD:
MEDIEVAL
ART

JAMES BARTER

LUCENT BOOKS

An imprint of Thomson Gale, a part of The Thomson Corporation

THOMSON

GALE

Detroit • New York • San Francisco • San Diego • New Haven, Conn. • Waterville, Maine • London • Munich

© 2006 Thomson Gale, a part of The Thomson Corporation.

Thomson and Star Logo are trademarks and Gale and Lucent Books are registered trademarks used herein under license.

For more information, contact
Lucent Books
27500 Drake Rd.
Farmington Hills, MI 48331-3535
Or you can visit our Internet site at http://www.gale.com

LIBRARY OF CONGRESS CATALOGING-IN-PUBLICATION DATA

Barter, James, 1946–
  In the glory of God : medieval art / by James Barter.
    p. cm.— (The Lucent library of historical eras. Middle Ages)
  Includes bibliographical references and index.
  Contents: Thoughts constructed in stone—Sculpted sermons—Painted icons—Biblical stories in tile and glass—Art to celebrate the mass—Painted prayers.
  ISBN 1-59018-862-4 (hard cover : alk. paper) 1. Art, Medieval. 2. Christian art and symbolism—Europe—Medieval, 500–1500. I. Title.
N7850.B37 2006
704.9'4820902—dc22
                                                                      2005029062

Printed in China

Contents

Foreword

Looking back from the vantage point of the present, history can be viewed as a myriad of intertwining roads paved by human events. Some paths stand out—broad highways whose mileposts, even from a distance of centuries, are clear. The events that propelled the rise to power of Germany's Third Reich, its role in World War II, and its eventual demise, for example, are well defined and documented.

Other roads are less distinct, their route sometimes hidden from view. Modern legislatures may have developed from old tribal councils, for example, but the links between them are indistinct in places, open to discussion and interpretation.

The architecture of civilization—law, religion, art, science, and government—as well as the more everyday aspects of our culture—what we eat, what we wear—all developed along the historical roads and byways. In that progression can be traced every facet of modern life.

A broad look back along these roads reveals that many paths—though of vastly different character—seem to converge at a few critical junctions. These intersections are those great historical eras that echo over the long, steady course of human history, extending beyond the past and into the present.

These epic periods of time are the focus of Lucent's Library of Historical Eras. They shine through the mists of history like beacons, illuminated by a burst of creativity that propels events forward—so bright that we, from thousands of years away, can clearly see the chain of events leading to the present.

Each Lucent Library of Historical Eras consists of a set of books that highlight various aspects of these major eras. For example, the Elizabethan England library features volumes on Queen Elizabeth I and her court, Elizabethan theater, the great playwrights, and everyday life in Elizabethan London.

The mini-library approach allows for the division of each era into its most significant and most interesting parts and the exploration of those parts in depth. Also, social and cultural trends as well as illustrative documents and eyewitness accounts can be prominently featured in individual volumes.

Lucent's Library of Historical Eras presents a wealth of information to young readers. The lively narrative, fully documented primary and secondary source quotations, maps, photographs, sidebars, and annotated bibliographies serve as launching points for class discussion and further research.

In studying the great historical eras, students also develop a better understanding of our own times. What we learn from the past and how we apply it in the present may shape the future and may determine whether our era will be a guiding light to those traveling future roads.

Introduction

ART INSPIRED BY FAITH

Amid the poverty, rampant disease, and incessant warfare that plagued the early medieval period (A.D. 500–1000), the prospect of better lives appeared dim to most people. The only optimism available to the suffering masses came from the Christian Church, which promised better times in the afterlife. Attaining entry into the kingdom of heaven, however, was contingent upon people's willingness to follow the Church's teachings, which stressed, among other things, the veneration of God.

Praising God took many more forms than simply the prayerful expressions that arose each Sunday from thousands of churches across Europe. Medieval artists and craftspeople created many pieces of art that served as outward expressions of inner spiritual devotion. Architects, sculptors, painters, stained-glass and mosaic designers, calligraphers, metalworkers, and weavers fashioned works of decorative spiritual art that can still be seen today.

Church leaders fostered the conviction that art should serve the Church. Paramount to medieval Christians was the belief that a close relationship existed between God's creativity and human creativity. Because God had created people, the medieval mind reasoned, art created by people was an extension of God. In effect, artistic creations were just one generation removed from the ultimate creator of all things. This viewpoint was expressed by the Italian writer Dante Alighieri, who noted in his epic poem *The Divine Comedy* in the early fourteenth century that art is the child of

The ornate splendor of cathedrals served to highlight the importance of the Church during the Middle Ages. Pictured here is an altar found in a fourteenth-century Italian cathedral.

God, stating, "Your art deserves the name of second in descent from God."[1]

During the one thousand years between 500 and 1500, known to historians as the Middle Ages, Western artists created religious masterpieces almost exclusively to be displayed in churches. Therefore, medieval art objects, whether wrought from common stone, wood, or glass or fashioned from exotic ivory, gems, or gleaming gold, nearly always expressed Christian themes. Artists were given free reign to execute their works but not to choose their compositions. This attitude was made clear as early as 787 at a Church council held in Nicaea, situated in the northern region of modern Turkey. That council affirmed, "The composition of religious imagery is not left to the initiative of the artists, but is formed upon principles laid down by the Catholic Church and by religious tradition."[2]

Unlike the art of preceding cultures as well as those that followed, medieval art was not distributed throughout villages and cities. Nor was it publicly collected for display in museums or privately gathered for personal enjoyment or prestige. To see art, and to absorb its spiritual themes, all medieval peoples, regardless of social position or personal wealth, were obligated to attend church. In fact, across Europe churches became the sole repositories of art.

Today, Christian art remains a major source of historical information for understanding the medieval period. In addition to their dual role as houses of worship and repositories of art, cathedrals have become places where scholars as well as the public can study and gather insights into the medieval Christian mind. And when they depart, modern visitors will have acquired some understanding of the significant role that art played in the religious lives of people more than a thousand years ago.

Chapter One

THOUGHTS CONSTRUCTED IN STONE

Students of history associate each great historical era with its major architectural monuments. The Egyptians built the pyramids, the Greeks their Parthenon, and the Romans the Colosseum. The great architectural statement of the Middle Ages is thousands of churches and cathedrals. In the opinion of medieval historian Emile Mâle: "Never has art summed up the thought of an age with such magnificence. The cathedral was the open book, in which people could learn all that was necessary for them to know. . . . The spectacle of these cathedrals, with their thousand images arising at the same moment in the great cities of France, is one of the wonders of history."[3]

Educating parishioners in the traditions of the Church was essential to the practice of worshipping God. Since most of these parishioners were illiterate, the works of art that filled churches and cathedrals functioned as visual aids to teach them about Christianity. Religious art's educational value is noted by Mâle, who states, "The cathedral is a book of thoughts where the pious come to learn."[4] Long before cosmopolitan civic and religious leaders constructed towering cathedrals filled with ornate works of art, however, people with simpler thoughts of their salvation built small, plain places of worship far from population centers.

The Early Architecture of Solitude

Immediately after the collapse of the Roman Empire at the end of the fifth century, before the hierarchy of the Church developed, devout men entering the church had two choices for spiritual service. One was to serve as a parish priest, living in the midst of a local population and ministering to its spiritual needs. The other was to live a hermitlike existence behind a walled monastery in a remote location. Men who chose this path, collectively known as monks, believed a life of isolation, poverty, and simplicity was the only true means for the salvation of one's soul. Saint Jerome, one of the early monks, issued this admonition to aspiring monks: "If you wish to perform the office of a priest, then live in cities and townships, and make the salvation of others the gain of your soul. But if you desire to be called a monk, which is solitary, what are you doing in cities, which are after all the dwelling places not of solitaries, but of the many?"[5]

In keeping with Saint Jerome's directive, monks gathered in small communities to live in hundreds of monasteries scattered across Europe. The purpose of their existence was captured in the simple Latin phrase *orare et laborare*, meaning "to pray and to work." The obligation to pray occupied more hours of the day than did the obligation to work, necessitating construction of buildings exclusively for meditation and prayer. In the opinion of Saint Jerome, "Let those of us who care for what is within . . . erect for their own use buildings conceived according to our pledge for prayer, taking holy simplicity as a model."[6]

The commitment to simplicity and prayer was reflected in monastic architecture. The monastic compound typically consisted of spartan buildings such as an unadorned chapel, dormitory, dining room, meeting hall, and a cloister, a

Notre Dame in Paris is considered by many historians to be the finest example of medieval architecture.

The stone buildings seen here are the ruins of an ancient monastery in western Ireland. They are typical of the Spartan simplicity of early monastic communities.

garden surrounded by walkways. Heavy stones held together by mortar imparted a somber look to monasteries: Beauty was not a consideration during the early Middle Ages. All buildings were connected by walkways on which Christian stories were frequently depicted in paint or set in stone to assist monks with their prayers as they strolled silently from place to place with their heads bowed.

The typical chapel, a small, blocky, graceless structure with an interior height rarely exceeding 30 feet (9m), reflected the seriousness of purpose within. Windows consisted of small glassless slits that let in little light. To widen the windows would weaken the walls and run the risk of their collapse under the weight of the roof. The darkness discouraged the monks

from looking around and thus being distracted from their silent prayer. Even fireplaces for providing winter warmth were banned to prevent monks from becoming comfortable enough to fall asleep. Because of the darkness and monastic vows of simplicity, interior decorations were shunned.

The other major buildings were similarly stark, small, and bare of decorations. The dormitory, in which monks slept, was a rectangular, one-story stone building without partitions but with windows for fresh air and a fireplace for heat. Likewise, the dining hall was a bleak place where monks ate collectively in silence at wooden benches and tables while one selected member read prayers aloud.

Thoughts Constructed in Stone   13

Pilgrims and Cathedrals

The abundance of Romanesque churches across Europe was partly a result of a phenomenon called pilgrimages, lengthy journeys taken by Christians to visit holy shrines at various cities throughout Europe and the Holy Land. Major cities containing important relics were Jerusalem; Constantinople (modern-day Istanbul, Turkey); Canterbury, England; Rome, Italy; Paris, France; and Santiago de Compostela, Spain.

A pilgrimage on foot might take several months. Stopover places in the form of churches where pilgrims could pause to pray, eat, and sleep sprang up across Europe. Many churches were built along established main roads to accommodate and profit from pilgrims. And whenever possible, many churches acquired real or counterfeit relics of their own to encourage pilgrim traffic to stop and spend money.

Each church tried to acquire at least one ancient relic associated with the life of Christ. The most revered were those known to have been touched by him, such as one of the nails from his cross, a piece of the cross, a piece of a garment once worn by him, and hundreds of incidental items Christ was alleged to have held. Art historian Leslie Ross explains in her book, *Artists of the Middle Ages*, that pilgrimages to see and pray before relics were undertaken "in order to worship, seek spiritual aid or physical healing, or to fulfill a vow or obligation."

In spite of the singularly monotonous and remote existence in monasteries, monks attracted the attention of travelers and local villagers. Some visitors were curiosity seekers inquisitive about the monks' unusual devotion to *orare et laborare*. Others sought spiritual guidance from esteemed monks, while the poor arrived each morning at the gates begging for leftover food. Because of these unwelcome interruptions, many monks set out to build monasteries even more remote so that no visitors could disrupt their unique lives.

Monasteries on Greek Mountain Tops

These monks found the perfect isolated location in central Greece, where dozens of stone pinnacles rose abruptly a thousand feet (300m) above the valley below. Because the tops of the peaks were accessible only by scaling the vertical rock bases, they were an ideal place in which to pray free from intruders. Hermit monks brought food up with them so they would not need to make the climb more than once every two weeks. By the eighth century this region, called Meteora, a Greek word meaning "hovering in air," had become one of Europe's most spectacular sacred sites.

By the ninth century, many individual monks began to work together to build simple structures on the tops of several peaks. They hauled up wood, bark, and other lightweight building materials and used them to construct basic shelters and places for worship. Because these monks were unable to hoist heavier permanent materials such as stone, brick, and concrete, their architecture was far simpler than that of their brethren living in monasteries below.

As time passed, more monks joined the dozen or so communities, and the need to expand grew. Although still lacking easy access, the simple structures nonetheless evolved into more complex monasteries that eventually numbered twenty-four. Soon, the monks built elaborate systems of winches and pulleys attached to baskets to lift small quantities of permanent building materials to the peaks. Because it was still difficult to hoist these dense materials, however, monasteries remained small and simple.

This simple architecture proved to be short-lived. Eventually, the majority of young men entering the Church chose to be parish priests, not hermit monks. For that reason, modest parish churches in small towns and large elegant cathedrals in major cities set the architectural tone for religious buildings in Europe for the next several centuries.

Romanesque Architecture

The beginning of the eleventh century witnessed an explosion of a new form of church architecture. The year 1000 had been awaited with great trepidation, as the belief spread throughout Europe that it would be the one in which Christ would return to earth and begin the Apocalypse that would end the world. But when the dreaded year came and went without calamity, a renewed sense of enthusiasm for life and spiritual faith

Mountaintop monasteries in Greece, such as this one in Thessaly, enabled monks to live in absolute isolation.

flowered. Certain that their lives would go on, optimistic builders produced a spate of architecture. The eleventh-century monk Raoul Glaber noted the construction boom in 1030:

So on the threshold of the aforesaid thousandth year, some two or three years after it, it befell almost throughout the world, but especially in Italy and Gaul [modern France], that the fabrics of churches were rebuilt. . . . So it was as though the very world had shaken herself and cast off her old age, and was clothing herself everywhere in a white garment of churches.[7]

The "white garment," as Glaber termed it, consisted of more than fifteen hundred churches that were constructed during the eleventh century in France, along with hundreds more in Italy and other countries. Because these churches were designed to be similar to structures built by the Romans, the style in which they were built became known as Romanesque.

The replication of Roman architecture meant that these churches' most common features were rounded stone arches and vaults—arching interior ceilings—and massive stone walls to carry the weight down to the foundation. Entrances were generally two side-by-side doors,

The façade of the Duomo in Pisa features the heavy masonry and narrow vertical windows that are characteristic of Romanesque architecture.

and windows were little more than a few narrow vertical slits that let in a small amount of daylight and were filled with glass to keep out winter winds.

Far from being elegant, Romanesque churches had a heavy, blocky appearance that was sometimes more forbidding than welcoming. This style suited the period, however, during which warfare frequently forced peasants to flee from their flimsy wood hovels to seek protection inside their churches. Under such brutish circumstances, beauty and elegance were secondary considerations to strength and an intimidating appearance.

Within one hundred years, the Romanesque style evolved to incorporate Christian symbols. Those entering a Romanesque church walked up the nave, a long center section that intersected at a right angle with a second, slightly shorter section called the transept. Viewed from above, the two large intersecting aisles formed a distinctive cross, a reminder of Christ's crucifixion. This design was known as the Roman cross, to differentiate it from the Greek cross, which had a nave and transept of equal lengths. Just beyond the intersection of the two aisles, which is called the crossing, stood the altar.

As the design continued to evolve, a tower was typically built precisely above the crossing to symbolize the physical point at which the spirit of God descended from heaven and entered the church. Over time, towers increased in height to symbolize reaching closer to heaven and the presence of God.

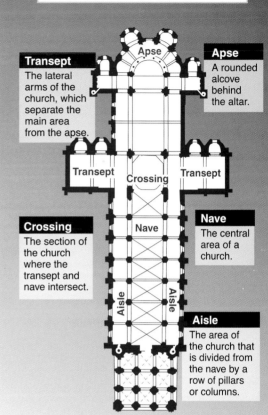

Roman Cross Architectural Design

Transept
The lateral arms of the church, which separate the main area from the apse.

Apse
A rounded alcove behind the altar.

Apse

Transept   Crossing   Transept

Crossing
The section of the church where the transept and nave intersect.

Nave

Nave
The central area of a church.

Aisle   Aisle

Aisle
The area of the church that is divided from the nave by a row of pillars or columns.

By the middle of the twelfth century, political and economic shifts ushered in an entirely new architectural form. As local wars subsided, economies improved, and stable legal systems took hold, people's sense of security was reflected in the design of their churches and cathedrals. The greater optimism of the times gave rise to a revolutionary form of architecture known as Gothic.

Gothic Architecture

Gothic architecture was in stark contrast to Romanesque. Whereas Romanesque churches appeared squat and closed-in with their stout stone walls, dark interiors, and low vaults, Gothic examples were characterized by taller vaults, thinner walls, and interiors flooded with colorful light streaming through stained-glass windows. Modern art historians regularly describe the Gothic form in terms such as elegant, graceful, beautiful, and refined.

The name *Gothic* was not applied to the new architectural form until the sixteenth century. At that time, Renaissance artists used the term derisively to imply it was the crude work of the Goths, barbarians from eastern Germany who had once swept across Europe destroying everything in their path. Renaissance artists believed the most beautiful architectural forms were Romanesque ones simply because their style more faithfully followed the techniques developed by the Romans.

The key to the advance of Gothic architecture was the use of pointed rather than rounded arches. Although the arched roofs used in Romanesque construction were an improvement over flat ones because the arch directed the weight of the roof outward and down to the walls, the height of the curves of these arches was limited to half the width of their bases. Anything taller was in danger of collapse. Gothic architects, however, used pointed arches that more efficiently transferred weight down to the ground. This allowed them to build taller churches with more expansive vaults. The Gothic cathedral in Beauvais, France, for example, towered 158 feet (48m) above

the floor, twice the height of the tallest Romanesque cathedral.

Enlarging the vaults and increasing the height of walls created dark cavernous interiors. Because no number of candles, not even thousands, could properly light them, glass windows were added to flood the interiors with daylight. Success with glass was not immediate, however—too much glass weakened the walls, causing them to buckle and explode outward under the weight of the roof. To solve this problem, architects eventually began adding heavy stone buttresses on the outside of the walls to reinforce them.

Once buttressing was applied, builders could add great banks of glass to cathedral walls. Colored glass, commonly called stained glass, was used to depict biblical stories in brilliant colors. These works delighted parishioners and, more importantly, educated those incapable of reading the Bible. Favorite subjects included the Creation of Adam and Eve, the Flood and Noah's Ark, the Birth of Christ, the Last Judgment, and the Crucifixion. These stories expressed in glass, in addition to other architectural features and works of art, helped create an atmosphere in which everything reflected an aspect of Christianity. Historian Tim Dowley writes:

Theology was reflected in the structure of the building; the upward striving towards God; the cross-shape; and the altar situated in the East, facing Jerusalem. Every detail of the creed—from the Trinity to the creation, and from the passion

Stained Glass and the Flying Buttress

The most celebrated innovation that transformed Romanesque architecture into Gothic was the magnificence of stained-glass windows. As Gothic cathedrals competed to be the tallest and most splendid, solid stone walls needed to support the massive weight of roofs gave way to increasing numbers and styles of colorful glass.

The use of stained glass was a direct consequence of the technical achievements of Gothic architects and engineers. Engineers learned from trial and error that buckling walls of cathedrals with large numbers of stained-glass windows needed to be supported. To remedy the problem, engineers designed the flying buttress.

Flying buttresses stabilized cathedral walls on the outside, out of view of worshippers within. Constructed of stone blocks and cement, they took the form of an arch or half arch connected to a cathedral wall at one end and a heavy stone pier firmly set in the ground a short distance away at the other end. To build a flying buttress, a temporary wooden form called a centering was first built by carpenters. The centering was the exact size and arc as would be required for the final stone buttress. The centering was used to support the weight of the stones as they were being set and maintain the precise shape of the arch until the cement in between each block hardened. Following one month during which time the cement hardened, the centering was removed. As Gothic cathedrals grew in height and walls acquired more stained-glass windows, two and in a few rare cases three flying buttresses were constructed one above the other to prevent the walls from buckling under the pressure of the roof.

Flying buttresses support the massive weight of the stone walls of Notre Dame's apse.

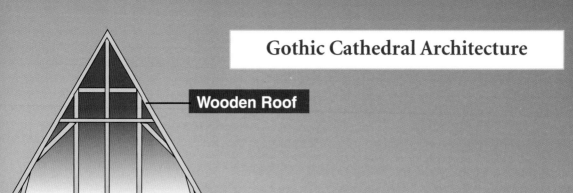

Gothic Cathedral Architecture

Wooden Roof

Pinnacle
Counter-balances the base

Flying Buttress
Supports walls of main structure

Pier Buttress
Supports the side aisle vaulting

Pointed Vaulting
Provides additional strength and stability

Side Aisle

of Christ to the Last Judgment—appeared in sculpture and stained glass. The harmony represented by such a structure signified the ideals of medieval art and thought.[8]

Perfection of the Gothic cathedral triggered a competition to see which city could praise God with the most impressive structure. Medieval historian Anne Fremantle describes a building boom in cathedrals that erupted in the thirteenth century:

Bishops and towns everywhere competed to produce the grandest, tallest edifices. Siena looked at the Duomo

The Drawings of Villard de Honnecourt

Few medieval manuscripts compiled by medieval architects have survived the centuries, making that of Villard de Honnecourt particularly important. Honnecourt was a thirteenth-century architect who wandered from town to town throughout much of northern and central France sketching architectural details of old and contemporary churches and cathedrals. His manuscript, which was not discovered until the mid-nineteenth century, comprises thirty-three vellum leaves made from pigskins and contains approximately 250 drawings.

The subjects of Honnecourt's drawings and inscriptions fall into several categories of architectural interest. He seemed to enjoy sketching details such as the sculpture above entry doors, sculptured animals, and carpentry. Also of interest was the engineering of churches.

Thirteenth-century architect Villard de Honnecourt sketched these flying buttresses at Reims Cathedral in northern France.

Several pages of drawings provide details of scaffolding used during construction, surveying techniques, and mechanical devices used to raise materials from the ground up to roofs.

Honnecourt's portfolio is a unique and valuable artifact. From it modern scholars have learned something of the life and interests of thirteenth-century architects, as well as thirteenth-century engineering and building techniques.

[cathedral] in Florence and decided to convert its own church into a mere transept for a cathedral. Notre Dame in Paris raised a vault 114 feet [35m]. Chartres surpassed it with 123 feet [37m] only to be surpassed by Reims with 124 feet [37.5m] and Amiens with 138 feet [42m]. Beauvais, jealous of Amiens, aimed 19 feet [6m] higher but the vault collapsed.[9]

When the competition finally settled toward the end of the fourteenth century, the majesty of one cathedral stood above all others. In the opinion of nearly every observer, the city of Chartres, 50 miles (83km) southwest of Paris, had constructed the finest. Elegant and inspiring in all respects, it quickly acquired a reputation as the queen of Gothic cathedrals.

The Queen of Gothic Cathedrals

When Chartres Cathedral was consecrated in 1260, sixty-six years after the groundbreaking, the bishop officiating over the ceremony made clear the cathedral's purpose when he said, "This is a place of awe. Here is the court of God and the gate of heaven."[10] Art historians today may not agree with the bishop's sentiments, but they widely consider this cathedral to be Europe's quintessential example of Gothic architecture.

Situated on the highest hill in the city, above the Eure River, the cathedral stood as a welcome beacon for weary travelers journeying on foot between Paris and destinations to the south in the Loire Valley. From miles in all directions caravans of

The stained glass windows (right) of Chartres Cathedral (below) in France are widely regarded as the most magnificent examples of stained glass ever produced.

Notable Medieval Cathedrals

England

York
Canterbury
Salisbury

Germany
Cologne
Strasbourg
Freiburg

Atlantic
Ocean

Amiens
Reims
Notre Dame
Chartres

France

Italy
Pisa
Florence
Siena

León

Spain

Toledo

Seville

Mediterranean Sea

EUROPE
ASIA
AFRICA

N
W   E
S

travelers looked for its single simple spire that rose 349 feet (106m) above the stone square below. Many years later, a second, more ornate and taller spire was added that surpassed the height of the first one by 28 feet (8m). Many cathedrals had two identical spires. What made those at Chartres distinctive was that the two spires were very different both in height and design.

The feature that brought the most fame to Chartres Cathedral, however, was its exceptionally large and beautiful array of stained-glass windows. Since the Middle Ages, they have been regarded as the finest examples of stained glassmaking ever produced. The dominant colors found in the thousands of individual pieces of stained glass are royal blue, red, yellow, and green, with blue as the dominant tint. Speaking about the glass of Chartres, medieval historian Gerald L. Browning expressed the view that "this was the message of God, delivered in the translucent gloom of a great church, reflected in a spectrum of colors spilling out of the naves and transepts, and settling like heavenly dust on all who walked within."[11]

As architecture emerged as the dominant medieval art form, sculpture grew as well. Cathedrals, both Romanesque and Gothic, provided sculptors with stone entryways, columns, and dozens of other architectural features to adorn. Church fathers ordered these surfaces carved with biblical scenes familiar and sacred to their congregations.

Chapter Two

SCULPTED SERMONS

As Romanesque and Gothic churches grew ever taller and larger, they provided sculptors with a virtually limitless number of stone surfaces to carve. Major architectural features became prime locations for sculpted depictions of biblical scenes. In this regard, cathedrals presented sermons in stone that could be understood by illiterate parishioners. Church leaders commissioned sculptors to cover interiors with carved renderings of Christian themes intended to overwhelm worshippers with a sense of awe for their creator and to express the glory of God.

The subjects expressed in stone tended to be the same from place to place. Travelers journeying to southern Italy, northern Sweden, Wales to the west, and Russia to the east could count on seeing the same themes repeated wherever they wandered. Scenes most often reproduced depicted the major events in the life of Christ—his birth in Bethlehem, baptism by John the Baptist, crucifixion, removal from the cross, ascension into heaven, and prophesied last judgment of all souls at world's end.

The consistency of themes was due in part to tradition and in part to the crews of sculptors who traveled from cathedral to cathedral carving on them. The construction of thousands of parish churches and dozens of major cathedrals throughout Europe was a boon to sculptors for generations. Working from dawn to dusk, these craftspeople outlined the same favored scenes and chiseled the forms. Once their work was completed they packed up their tools, loaded them on carts, and headed down the road in search of the next town with a recently constructed church.

Medieval sculptors found inspiration from thousands of years of Greek and then Roman masters. Many medieval

Sculptures of biblical scenes, like this crucifixion scene from a cathedral in Germany, served to educate medieval Europe's largely illiterate parishioners.

carvers traveled to Rome and other leading cities once within the sweep of the Roman Empire to study the craft of their predecessors. Once there, they also learned how to make a variety of chisels, outline the forms they intended to carve, and perfect techniques for high-quality renderings.

Art historians place medieval sculpture into three fundamental categories. The earliest and most rudimentary is called low relief and is most often associated with the Romanesque period. When Gothic architecture emerged, low relief gave way to high relief, which was more befitting the larger and more ornate cathedrals of that period. And finally, three-dimensional, also commonly called "freestanding," sculpture emerged as the most highly refined form of medieval sculpture.

Low-Relief Sculpture

Early medieval sculptural forms were carved out of flat stone surfaces. Known as low-relief sculpture, these forms extended only 1 to 3 inches (2.5 to 7.5cm) outward from the background. The term *relief* refers to the fact that the forms project out from, or are relieved from, their flat background. Although relatively simple, low-relief carvings represented a significant transition from etchings and engravings, which are two-dimensional and lack any measurable depth at all.

Low-relief carving was frequently the only method possible because many stone surfaces desirable for carving were no more than 6 inches (15cm) thick.

Walls supporting heavy roofs might be many feet thick, but high-profile areas that would catch the eye of worshippers were usually made of long, broad, thin slabs. Because they were flat and easily cracked, these surfaces were placed on long wooden benches, then sketched by sculptors, carved no deeper than half their thickness, winched into place on a sturdy wall, and finally fixed in place with a layer of concrete.

Low-relief sculpture, by its nature, created visual limitations for viewers. Lacking much depth, these works were viewable only from the front. As observers moved to either side, the flatness of the works caused them seemingly to fade into

A number of detailed sculptures of Jesus and his apostles appear on the façade of this cathedral in southern France.

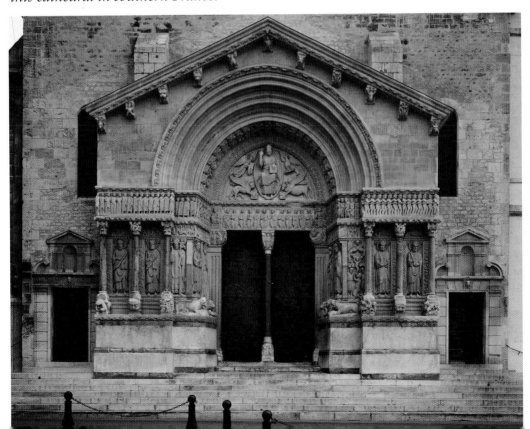

Gislebertus

Many examples of medieval sculpture exist, yet few of their creators are known. One, however, the twelfth-century French sculptor Gislebertus, is known because of his many sculptural contributions to the Cathedral of Saint Lazare in the city of Autun. This cathedral was a favorite place for pilgrims to visit because it supposedly housed the bones of Lazarus who, according to biblical tradition, Jesus miraculously raised from the dead.

Gislebertus was commissioned to carve sculptures for several doorways, tympanums, and column capitals that represent some of the best work of this period. Of his many contributions to the Cathedral of Saint Lazare, the one that was most renowned at that time was the tympanum over the main entrance. This complex work representing the Last Judgment was carved from several large slabs of limestone quarried in the nearby hills.

Gislebertus also carved four scenes depicting various biblical descriptions of the Three Wise Men. On one, he had to include all three in a small space. He cleverly devised a scene showing the three men crowded together in bed under just one blanket. The blanket is an extension of the wings of an angel that hovers above the sleeping men. With one hand the angel points to the star that will guide them to the baby Jesus in Bethlehem.

their backgrounds. The other drawback to this sculptural form was a lack of depth of field—depicting one object to appear far away in the background and another close by in the foreground was nearly impossible.

Low-relief biblical sculpture common to Romanesque architecture reflected the psychology of that dismal period. At a time when warfare, disease, and poverty were common, depression and despair were a part of everyone's life. These emotions were visible in low-relief sculptures that depicted religious figures closely packed together, with stiff bodies and faces void of expression. In the opinion of art historian Mâle: "Many carved faces share the identical blank stare. . . . Joyless in their lack of eye contact with those entering [the church], their stark appearances seem intended to ward off worshippers rather than welcome them in."[12]

Church Portals

These figures often were carved onto the flat surface above the main portals. Passing from the world of day-to-day secular activities into the more somber world of spiritual ceremony was intended to impart a dramatic and emotional change of focus on Sunday. To remind parishioners immediately of the necessity of conducting pious lives and to focus their thoughts on subjects appropriate for church as they entered, builders placed a dramatic piece of sculpture immediately above the portals in a semicircular area called the tympanum. The tympanums of large cathedrals spanned their double and sometimes triple door entries, covering as much as 50 feet (15m). Each entry had its own individual tympanum, and each was an essential component of the entire sculpture.

The most powerful and commonly sculptured theme for tympanums was the Last Judgment of Christ, referred to by art historian H.W. Janson as "the most awesome scene in Christian art."[13] This scene shows the end of the world as predicted by the Bible, when Christ returns to earth to pass judgment on all souls. Some souls he will send to heaven, while others he will condemn to eternal hell.

The tradition of this sculptured work places Christ at the center, surrounded by angels. To his left and right are usually carved his mother, the Virgin Mary, and his twelve disciples. In the most dramatic

Found above the portal to a German cathedral, this incredibly detailed relief depicts dramatic scenes from the life of the Virgin Mary.

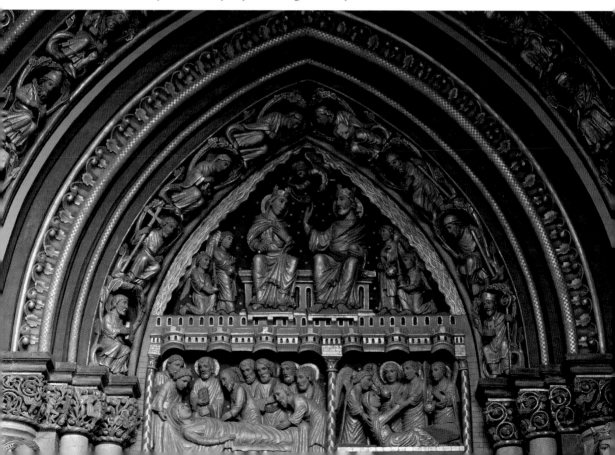

scene, a scale is depicted on which the souls are symbolically being weighed to determine their worthiness to enter heaven. Those that qualify are shown floating heavenward with serene expressions, while those that fail are depicted with expressions of terror as grotesque beasts with clawlike hands tear at their legs, pulling them down into hell. Amid the chaos, angels tug on one end of the scales filled with souls while the devil, depicted as a skeleton, pulls on the other. Typical of these Last Judgment scenes is the relatively small number of souls heaven-bound compared to the masses being dragged downward.

When parishioners looked up as they entered church on Sunday morning, each saw the graphic warning that choosing good behavior, as taught by the Christian Church, would be rewarded, while anyone who chose evil could expect to be condemned to hell for eternal punishment. Medieval art historian Mâle rhetorically poses this question: "Can any scene more agonizing be imagined? How could the spectator avoid being caught up in the anguish of those souls who waited with trembling for the moment when the scale would tip? Such was the first great lesson that sculpture taught: it went straight to the point."[14]

Low-relief sculpture was found inside the church as well as on the tympanum. Carvings on the altar, baptismal font, and ends of pews depicted less well-known religious scenes. As cathedrals transitioned from Romanesque to Gothic, however, sculpture advanced to high relief.

High-Relief Sculpture

Decorating sophisticated Gothic cathedrals meant abandoning the relatively flat, simplistic low-relief sculptural forms associated with Romanesque architecture. The soaring heights and elegant features of Gothic cathedrals challenged sculptors to carve in high relief, creating works that projected 4 to 8 inches (10 to 20cm) above the surface of their background. Some even displayed undercutting, the carving away of enough of the background stone to approach three-dimensionality and achieve greater anatomical realism. The height of these carvings was further accentuated by the shadows they cast as the sun moved across the sky.

This new sculptural form required a thick architectural feature such as a column capital, the stone section that sat between a column and the stone work above it, called the entablature. Free-standing capitals were initially sculpted in the tradition of the Greeks and Romans, with acanthus leaves and other flowery designs. Later, however, sculptured capitals depicted religious subjects such as the faces of the apostles, the Garden of Eden, and Christ preaching in the Garden of Gethsemane.

Pilasters were another favored location for high-relief sculptures. Pilasters were similar to columns, but projected out from a wall at the corners. They provided sculptors with a surface that could be carved to reveal a three-quarter view—the front and two sides. Parishioners inside Gothic cathedrals enjoyed seeing

Sculptured Gargoyles

The desire to build the finest cathedrals inspired the ingenuity of all medieval craftspeople. The massive, ornate stained-glass windows, elaborate interior altars, and intricately sculptured doors and tympanums would not have survived to this day had medieval engineers failed to pay attention to the removal of potentially damaging rainwater from cathedral roofs.

Initially this water was discharged through lead pipes to the courtyards below. But with the transition from Romanesque to Gothic architecture, something more decorative than drainpipes was needed.

Gothic craftspeople opted instead for elaborately sculptured stone gargoyles, a term from the early French language meaning "throat." For reasons not clearly understood today, gargoyles were often carved to represent bizarre and monstrous scary forms, such as half-man–half-beast creatures and people tormented by the fangs and claws of wild animals. Each of the dozens of gargoyles created for a cathedral was unique.

One gargoyle on the roof of Notre Dame devours a smaller beast while another looks out over the city of Paris.

the frontal view of faces as they approached and the profiles as they passed by. Never before had sculptors depicted ears, noses, and eyes as seen from the side, nor chins projecting out from the face. Because they were three-sided, renderings of arms, legs, hands, and feet appeared more realistic as well. Moreover, three-quarter sculpting of faces allowed for more emotional and individualized expressions, and these expressions reflected the greater optimism of the times. Wide smiles, looks of wonder, sidelong glances, and heads tilted in different directions were all possible in high-relief carvings.

As high relief reached its zenith in the early fourteenth century, figures became so realistic they appeared almost as if they might suddenly step away from cathedral walls into the aisles to join worshippers. One of the more well-known carvings on a pilaster can be found at Amiens Cathe- dral in France. It is a sculpture that shows Christ holding a crown in his outstretched hand, almost as if handing it to each person passing by.

Sculptured Columns

In addition to capitals and pilasters, columns were common locations for high-relief carvings, particularly the columns flanking the main doors. These carvings generally consisted of sculpted figures, called jamb figures, their bodies

Elaborate high-relief sculptures of figures and flowers crown the sandstone columns of a cathedral in Scotland.

The Golden Madonna in Crisis

The most well-known medieval sculpture formed from gold is the 2.5-foot-tall statue (0.76m) named the *Golden Madonna*. It is also the oldest known sculpture of the Virgin Mary in western Europe. It was commissioned in 990 in Essen, Germany, where it was the centerpiece of the cathedral's extensive collection of art. The sculpture depicts the Virgin Mary seated, holding an apple that symbolizes the original sin of Eve in the Garden of Eden.

Today more than one thousand years old, the famed statue is so fragile that art historians are afraid to handle it for fear of damaging it. Nonetheless, unless it is restored, it will continue to deteriorate. To determine why the statue is collapsing, computer tomography, a process used by doctors to scan the human body, was used. Following multiple scans, researchers discovered the problem. The creator of the statue constructed an inner structure made of wood that supported the layer of gold. Because the wood structure is rotting, it can no longer bear the weight of the gold.

The problem faced by art restorationists is how to repair the statue. A decision has not yet been made, but the two leading proposals are either to cut the statue open and replace the wood structure with another wooden one or replace it with a ceramic structure that will not rot.

slightly elongated to conform to the tall but narrow columns. They typically depicted religious personages reaching all the way back to the Old Testament, including prophets, martyrs, great teachers, bishops, monks, and even saintly kings and beggars. These sculptures were intentionally placed at cathedral portals to welcome parishioners on their way to worship. In the opinion of art historian Mâle: "Nothing is more impressive than the biblical statues which greet the visitor on the north portico of cathedrals. Abraham, Moses, Samuel, David, Isaiah, Jeremiah, Simon, St. John the Baptist, St. Peter fall one upon the other like the centuries, and relate the history of the world. The life of Christ is a culmination of this long history."[15]

Columns were carved in place after they had been set up. Sculptors were either given sketches to work from or had sculpted a particular saint so many times that they knew what characteristics and clothing identified that saint to the public. Saint Peter, for example, was always portrayed with the keys to heaven and the upside-down cross on which he was crucified. Saint James holds the club with which he was beaten to death, and Saint Veronica holds the handkerchief she offered to Christ.

Freestanding Sculpture

Contained within the art of high relief was the quest for true three-dimensionality, a quest that was achieved when sculptors freed their works from flat walls and columns to stand alone in open space. This revolutionary advance allowed sculptors to represent, in a single block of stone, an entire human figure, as he or she might appear in real life. Of greater importance, it permitted viewers to walk around the work and view it from all angles.

Sculptors who produced freestanding works created far more accurate representations of real-life objects than could their predecessors carving in relief. Because it allowed them to represent the human body as an articulated structure capable of expressing movement, this new form compelled artists to study human anatomy to understand how the position of one body part influences the positions of many others. As shoulders rotate, for example, so do the chest, arms, hips, and legs. Sculptors also experimented for the first time with multiple bodies intertwined with each other.

Medieval art historian H.W. Van Os sees powerful emotions expressed in medieval freestanding sculptures. In his book, *The Art of Devotion in the Late Middle Ages in Europe*, he discusses the emotional impact religious freestanding sculpture had on viewers:

All three-dimensional forms are perceived as having an expressive character as well as purely geometric properties. They strike the observer as delicate, aggressive, flowing, taut, relaxed, dynamic, soft, and so on. By exploiting the expressive qualities of form, medieval sculptors were able to create images in which subject matter and expressiveness of form were mutually reinforcing. Such images went beyond the mere presentation of biblical themes to communicate a wide range of subtle and powerful feelings.[16]

The Pietà

One of the most common and emotionally evocative subjects of freestanding sculpture was the moment, not recorded in the Bible, when Jesus's body was removed from the cross and placed on the lap of his grief-stricken mother, Mary. Known as the Pietà, a word meaning both "pity" and "piety," this scene was carved by dozens of medieval artists. In all portrayals of this poignant moment, Mary stares down sorrowfully at Christ's slumped, lifeless form.

By the thirteenth century, life-sized marble depictions of the Pietà could be viewed in major European cathedrals. Their emotionally gripping message about Christ's sacrifice for all humankind

Even the finest sculptors faced a daunting challenge when commissioned to carve a Pietà, a moving depiction of the Virgin Mary holding Jesus following his death.

was matched by the pathos of a heartbroken mother who has lost her son. The Pietà was intended to cause viewers to reflect on the sacrifices others made for their salvation and to give praise for their suffering. In the words of art historian Jan Mainzer: "This is a sculpture of Mary grieving and holding the dead Christ. It's an imagined scene that was meant to be an aid to devotion and an aid to one's personal meditations."[17]

Master sculptors considered a commission to carve a Pietà a monumental challenge. Unlike many other sculptures in the round, the Pietà required two human forms, intertwined, and the rendering of two facial expressions in such a way that viewers standing in front of the sculpture could see both at the same time.

Once a block of marble large enough for the project was secured, the sculptor began work by transferring a preliminary two-dimensional sketch to the three-dimensional block. Carving a monumental Pietà took between two and four years. Convention required that the spear wound in Christ's right side be visible to the viewer. Each sculptor also detailed the nail holes in Christ's hands and feet. Although in real life a man would gener-ally be larger than a woman, sculptors had to make Mary larger to prevent her from being lost beneath the sculpture of Christ.

After the front side of the stone was roughed out, the back was carved to show the back of Mary's body and one side of Christ as he reclines across her lap. Following the rough chiseling, finer chisels were used to create gaps that showed the separation of arms and legs, carve deep folds in clothing, and provide skeletal and muscle detail. The finest chisels were then used to add lines to faces, knuckles to fingers, and nails to toes. Lastly, a sculptor used a gritty stone substance called pumice to polish the marble.

The names of medieval sculptors whose works heightened worshippers' religious experiences are largely lost to art historians. That fact, however, does not diminish the contributions they made to their religion and to sculptors who followed and learned from their pioneering skills.

While sculpture flourished as a major decorative form for churches and cathedrals in western Europe, paintings proliferated in eastern Europe. Artists there painted both on wood panels and on the plaster of walls and ceilings to adorn their places of worship.

◆Chapter Three

PAINTED ICONS

Most medieval art created to praise God was produced in western Europe. Yet religious art was also being created in eastern Europe, principally in countries bordering the Aegean and eastern Mediterranean seas. Most art historians consider Greece, Turkey, and even a portion of western Russia the principal centers for what is known as Byzantine art. The term *Byzantine* was taken from the city of Byzantium (modern-day Istanbul, Turkey), the leading cultural center of eastern Europe from the sixth to the fifteenth centuries.

Byzantine artists produced one particular form of art better than did their counterparts in western Europe—paintings. Paintings in Byzantine monasteries and churches were generally of two types: works painted on flat wood panels, and frescoes, which were painted on walls and ceilings. Both forms of paintings are referred to as icons, a term taken from the Greek word meaning "image," or in these Christian cases, "holy images."

Icons are portraits of holy figures such as Jesus and Mary, along with disciples and well-known saints. Art historian Leslie Ross explains, "Generally speaking, when we think of an 'icon' we imagine the representation of a holy figure created in paint on a flat wood panel or wall."[18] According to tradition, icon painting began when Christ was carrying his cross to the crucifixion site and a woman named Veronica handed him her handkerchief to clean the sweat and blood from his face. Jesus wiped his face and returned the handkerchief to Veronica, leaving behind a permanently imprinted image of his face on the cloth. Although this incident does not appear in the Bible, early Christians often retold it.

Icons were more sacred than mere portraits. Art historians discussing the

Art of the Byzantine Empire

The Byzantine Empire, Sixth Century

North Atlantic Ocean

North Sea

RUSSIA

EUROPE

Paris

ASIA

Bay of Biscay

Ravenna

Black Sea

Córdoba

Adriatic Sea

Rome

Constantinople

Antioch

Carthage

Athens

SICILY

Mediterranean Sea

Alexandria

AFRICA

Jerusalem

Byzantine Icon Painting

Byzantine Fresco

Byzantine Mosaics

unique significance of icons typically make the point that icons were considered to have a direct mystical connection with the person they portrayed. Ross points out: "They are not 'just' portraits or pictures of people; they are not designed to amuse, delight, or entertain viewers. Instead, icons have an extremely serious religious function. An icon . . . establishes a connection between the sacred personage and the person praying before the image."[19]

Icons painted on wood panels are older and rarer than those painted on walls. Because wood cracks and decays easily, only a small percentage of these remain, held in churches and museums today. Nonetheless, enough have survived to provide modern-day scholars and students with a good sampling.

Painted Wood Panels

Few materials suitable for painting were available to medieval painters. The one most readily accessible and affordable was wood. As one unknown icon painter in the ninth century said, "I adore the material [wood] through which my salvation has come."[20] Dense-grained lime wood was favored, but poplar, cypress, and oak were also used. First, boards were planed and sanded until they were between 1 and 2 inches (2.5 and 5cm) thick. Because large boards warped easily, icons that were intended to be larger than 5 square feet (0.5sq. m) required two or more panels joined on the back side using iron clamps and wood bracing. Joining multiple wood panels to form one uniformly smooth surface limited wood icons to about 30 square feet (3sq. m).

The first step in preparing the painted side was for carpenters to create a slightly convex surface by recessing it away from the outer edge, which became the frame. The recessed surface was then smoothed and sanded to receive a chalk substance called gesso. This white priming material was applied to fill in any cracks, nicks, or irregularities on the wood surface. Gesso was applied and lightly sanded, one layer upon another, until a uniformly smooth white painting surface was created. When dry, it was given a final rubbing with coarse horsetail hair and handed to the painter.

Paints were not available for sale during medieval times. Part of the education of each apprentice painter was to learn the craft of making paints, a carefully guarded secret. The majority of pigments were derived from finely ground minerals. Vivid blues came from cobalt, azurite, and lapis lazuli. Malachite and verdigris produced greens, alkaline chromate produced orange, and porphyry and hematite made reds. Dried and pulverized insects, roots, flowers, and shellfish provided other colors. Painters combined powdered pigments with egg yolks, which functioned to bind the ingredients together.

Painters prided themselves on their ability to create brilliant colors that would not be found elsewhere. One way to accomplish this was to locate sources of paints unknown to other painters. The

Eggs and Artists

Without eggs, medieval paintings might have been disappointing. Artists manufactured paints, called tempera, by mixing finely ground pigment, water or vinegar, and egg yolk. The word *tempera* derives from the Latin word *temperare*, which means to blend or mix. Eggs were used as the binding agent that held the ingredients of the paint together.

Egg-based tempera was the primary medium for painters beginning in the eleventh century until the sixteenth century, when it was replaced by oil-based paints. The combination of egg yolk and powdered pigment created paint that in the case of some icons has lasted more than a thousand years.

Egg-based tempera paint had other characteristics that interested painters. Its ability to dry quickly was important because painters liked to add several layers of paint, each of which had to dry before the next could be applied. The use of multiple layers allowed the paint to express distinct properties, depending upon the look the painter wished to achieve. Tempera can be used as an opaque color, created by a thick application of several layers of a single tone. It can also be used to produce opalescence, a rainbow effect made by applying lighter tones over darker tones.

late medieval painter Cennino Cennini tells this story about collecting rare minerals: "Upon reaching a little valley, a very wild steep place, scraping it with a spade, I beheld seams of many kinds of color: ocher, dark and light, blue, and white, . . . and this I held the greatest wonder in the world—that white could exist in a seam in the earth."[21]

After the icon was outlined on the gesso with charcoal, the initial layers of paint were applied. The careful application of individual thin layers, each allowed to dry before the next was applied, gradually imparted a rich, deep quality to the figure. Finally, details such as an inscription,

facial lines and highlights, or folds in garments were added. Medieval artists frequently enhanced their works with gilding. To do this, they applied pieces of gold leaf, tiny sheets of gold thinner than tissue paper. Because gilding reflected flickering candlelight, it was used on parts of a painting that the artist wanted to highlight, such as a halo or angel's wings. When all paint had dried and the gold leaf was in place, the icon was sealed with a

A painted wood panel depicts Jesus with a halo. The gilding common to the era adds luster to the artwork.

coating of oil or varnish to protect it from candle soot, dust, and moisture.

Wood panel paintings did not appeal to artists interested in large icons with many holy images. These artists instead worked on entire walls and even domed ceilings. The technical skills needed for painting a fresco on a plaster surface were decidedly different from those needed to paint wood panels.

The Art of Fresco Painting

The unique quality of fresco painting is revealed by its name. The term *fresco* is an Italian word meaning "fresh" and refers to the fact that the paint is applied while the outer layer of plaster is still wet on the wall. When paint is applied to a wet wall or ceiling, it seeps deep into the plaster to create a permanent bond in which the painting becomes an integral part of the wall.

The first step for medieval artists involved mathematics and geometry. Crucial to a flawlessly executed fresco was to measure a wall perfectly, laying out the dimensions to be decorated. Precise calculations began with determining the area to be painted, locating

The walls and ceiling of a chapel in an Italian cathedral are adorned with brightly colored frescoes depicting biblical scenes.

dead-center points along both the vertical and horizontal lines of symmetry, and determining if the surface was perfectly plumb, meaning all walls joined the ceiling and floor at right angles. A final mathematical layout of the surface provided a geometric map for the precise positioning, balancing, and scaling to size of all figures to be painted on the fresco.

The first step in the actual painting was the outlining of all major figures. Some painters drew these figures freehand, while others created sketches on dried animal skin called vellum. They then perforated the outline with hundreds of pinpricks, held each individual piece of vellum in place, and tapped charcoal through the perforations. This technique left a charcoal mark on the dry plaster after the vellum was removed. When the entire fresco had been outlined with charcoal, the painter reviewed the totality at a distance to ensure proper spacing, proportions, and definition. Any necessary changes were then made.

The final step in completing the fresco was actually two steps that occurred almost simultaneously—applying the final wet coat of plaster followed immediately by the paint. Since the final application of plaster covered the charcoal outline, the painter applied it to small sections at a time, then quickly painted it. Areas requiring little detail, such as distant landscape scenes, could be completed in large sections in a matter of hours, whereas complex elements like a face might take an entire day.

Cimabue's Fresco of the Betrayal of Christ

One of the finest masters of fresco painting was the thirteenth-century artist Cimabue. During the 1260s, he was commissioned to paint a large number of works, most notably a series at a monastery in Assisi, Italy. Cimabue, whose real name was Cenni di Pepo or Peppi, painted few frescoes more exquisitely than the one in Assisi called the *Betrayal of Christ*, considered by many art historians to be the most dramatic panel in the monastery.

At the center of the fresco are Christ and Judas, one of his twelve apostles. The fresco depicts the moment near the end of Christ's life when Judas leans forward to kiss him on the cheek to identify him to Roman soldiers. According to the Bible, Judas was paid thirty silver coins to betray Christ, but when he did and then realized the consequences of his action, he threw away the silver coins and committed suicide.

Cimabue shows tension between the two men by portraying Christ looking away from Judas as the betrayer moves closer for the fateful kiss. Neither man smiles, suggesting that each is aware that the kiss is not an act of affection. Art historians writing about this icon are in general agreement that Cimabue painted it to juxtapose the goodness of Christ with the wickedness of Judas. The painting was expected to evoke great compassion for Christ as he is betrayed by one of his close friends and disdain for corrupt Judas, who deceives Christ out of greed.

Cimabue and other painters excelled at frescoes, but they were not affordable to all churches. Many church leaders eschewed large frescoes in favor of smaller, less expensive wood panels. For those that did, the compositions were typically focused on just one or two portraits well known to worshippers rather than the epic events more suitable for walls.

The Virgin Mary and the Christ Child

The most common portraits painted on wood icons were those of the Virgin Mary and the Christ Child. To the medieval Christian mind, Mary and Christ occupied the pinnacle of the Christian hierarchy. Contemporary art historians have cataloged thousands of wood panels bearing their likenesses in hundreds of churches from as far east as Russia to the western border of Europe.

Of the many variations of these icons, the one that was most widely reproduced was called *Mother of God Hodegetria.* *Hodegetria* is a Greek term meaning "guide of the way." According to tradition, the original *Mother of God Hodegetria* was painted on the surface of a family table by Saint Luke in 453. Hundreds of others followed between the fifth and fifteenth centuries.

This Russian Hodegetria *icon of the Virgin Mary and Jesus is from the fifteenth century.*

This icon depicts Mary holding the baby Christ on her left arm while she points to him with her right hand. Mary slightly bows her head in deference to the baby while fixing her stare out toward the viewer. In the opinion of art historians Konrad Onasch and Annemarie Schnieper, Mary's pose is intended to "invite the viewer to behold him [Christ]."[22]

In all of these icons, Christ has the small body of a baby but the head and facial features of a much older boy, and occasionally those of a young man. He sits tilting his head back a bit and looking up into his mother's eyes. He holds his right hand with the index and middle fingers extended while the others are

Creating Black Paint

To the trained eye of the medieval painter, no two black paints were the same. Painters often used several different kinds and shades of black and, therefore, needed to know several techniques for making this one color. Cennino Cennini, writing in his book, The Craftsman's Handbook, *around the late 1300s, discussed these techniques:*

Know that there are several kinds of black colors. There is black which is made from vine twigs; these twigs are to be burned; and when they are burnt, throw water on them, and quench them; and then work them up like the other black. And this is a color both black and lean and it is one of the perfect colors we employ. There is another black which is made from burnt almond shells or peach stones, and this is a perfect black. There is another black which is made in this manner; take a lamp full of linseed oil, and fill the lamp with this oil, and light the lamp. Then put it so lighted, underneath a good clean baking dish, and have the little flame of the lamp come to the bottom of the dish, two or three fingers away, and the smoke which comes out of the flame will strike on the bottom of the dish, and condense in a mass. Wait a while; take the baking dish, and with some implement sweep the color, that is, this soot, off on to a paper, or in some dish; and it does not need to be worked up or ground, for it is a very fine color.

---

folded into his palm. This gesture was a commonly understood sign of benediction, a blessing of peace and friendship toward others. In his left hand he holds a scroll representing the written rules of the church.

Icons as Instructional Stories

The *Mother of God Hodegetria* and other often-reproduced icons were intended primarily to instill parishioners with religious faith. Secondarily, they were painted to provide graphic representations of biblical stories for illiterate worshipers incapable of reading scripture. The sixth-century pope Gregory the Great recognized the value of icons used in this way and supported their production, noting that, "Painting can do for the illiterate what writing does for those that can read."[23]

Children grew up looking at icons in church while priests told a lengthy story associated with each one. By the time the children matured and had heard the story often repeated, a simple glance at the icon sufficed to remind them of its significance. The icon depicting a woman holding a handkerchief with the face of Christ on it, for example, told the story of Veronica, who aided the suffering Christ as he dragged himself toward his crucifixion.

Common folk expected each copy of a well-known icon to look the same regardless of where they might see it. Painters often took their art supplies to churches where venerated icons hung and could be copied. In the medieval view, following long-honored traditions was of greater value than innovation. H.W. Janson emphasized the importance of the conformity of icons, explaining, "Because of the veneration in which they were held, icons had to conform to strict formal rules, with fixed patterns repeated over and over again."[24] A major deviation from an old master icon could be as troublesome to illiterate worshippers as a major change to the text of the Bible would be to the literate.

An example of how a slight change in an icon can alter its meaning can be seen in the icons that portray Christ carrying a lamb. Some of these icons depict the lamb with a circular disk, or nimbus, above its head, while other icons depict the identical subject without the nimbus. Medieval worshippers knew that the lamb with the nimbus represented Christ as a young man in the company of God, his father. This demonstrates, according to art historian Alphonse Didron, "Christ and his father are one and the same." The lamb without the nimbus told an entirely different story. It symbolized Christ at an older age, just before his crucifixion. Didron explains, "Christ is represented as a human man, not God, who is aware that he will soon sacrifice his life on the cross."[25]

The significance of the addition or removal of a nimbus also highlights the important role that symbols played in the way messages were conveyed to parishioners. Instead of deliberately portraying some biblical figures, many icon painters chose instead to represent them with symbols.

Use of Christian Symbolism

Three of these figures were God, who was shown as a burning bush, the Holy Ghost, pictured as a dove swooping down from above, and Satan, who was depicted as a snake. Each symbol was derived from a biblical passage: In Exodus, Moses hears the voice of God coming from a burning bush; in Matthew, a dove appears above the head of Christ the moment he is baptized; and in Genesis, Satan assumes the form of a snake. Whenever painters included these symbols in their works, their significance was understood by everyone.

A second reason for the use of symbols was to represent the presence of a great spiritual being without detracting from the rest of the composition. Christ, for example, was often symbolically referred to in the Bible as the "lamb of God." Painters wishing to include his presence in a painting, yet focus the viewer's attention on some other person or theme, often painted a lamb in place of Christ himself.

The use of symbols was not the only clever strategy that painters developed to represent biblical scenes. A second, which took far longer to perfect than symbolism, was a pictorial language consisting of several visual deceptions that made paintings more realistic.

The Pictorial Language of Icons

Paintings possessed a complexity greater than other forms of medieval art except architecture. Although painters executed their icons on a two-dimensional flat plane, they used the innovative techniques of perspective and proportion, particularly toward the end of the medieval period, to make their sacred images seem almost three-dimensional.

Perspective is based on the optical principle that objects close to a viewer appear larger and more detailed than distant objects. To create perspective and make the proportions of a scene look realistic, painters placed small, undefined figures in the background and larger, more greatly detailed people in the foreground.

Proportion was a second technique used to impart realism. In some early icons, saints have body parts that are so out of proportion to each other that they appear

The perspective of this fifteenth-century Italian painting gives viewers the impression that the holy dove is flying in front of the people praying behind it.

Icon Painter Andrey Rublyov

Byzantine art historians widely consider the high-water mark of icon painting to have been achieved by the Russian painter Andrey Rublyov during the latter part of the fourteenth and early fifteenth centuries. At that time, Rublyov's reputation as an icon painter extended from Moscow to Paris.

Rublyov grew up near Moscow and as a teenager entered a nearby monastery. As a monk, Rublyov displayed a keen talent for painting and studied under master artists. By the time he was twenty, his teachers urged him to dedicate his energies to painting icons. Rublyov had a quiet and perceptive personality that suited him well for work that required total dedication to prayer and painting isolated from his colleagues in the monastery. In the opinion of art historians Konrad Onasch and Annemarie Schnieper, who specialize in icons, Rublyov's finest painting, depicting the face of Christ, resides in the Russian city of Zvenigorod. They describe it in their book, *Icons: The Fascination and*

Reality. "The face of Christ, painted in delicate, shaded, brown hues with deep-set eyes, and with a gentle gaze radiating tranquility and unsentimental kindness, is of such tender sensitivity that this portrait belongs to Andrey Rublyov, the most lyrical of all Russian icon painters."

The delicate portrayal of Christ in this icon by Andrey Rublyov reveals why many historians consider the Russian artist's work to be the pinnacle of icon art.

comical to the modern viewer. Toward the end of the Middle Ages, however, a group of Byzantine painters in Greece wrote a manual called the *Painter's Manual of Mount Athos*. In it they explained how to create proper proportion for the body using the head as a unit of measure: "The natural human being measures nine heads from forehead to the soles of the feet."[26] They also used the nose as the smallest unit of measurement, noting that the normal, head, from forehead to chin, was five noses long and that the distance from the hairline to eyes equaled two noses.

The finest painters used perspective and proportion to imitate nature more closely than ever before. Their fluid style featured long flowing brush strokes that accurately depicted the naturally occurring curves and lines of the human body. As a result, painted icons became one of the favored art forms during the Middle Ages. Other art forms emerged to rival them, however. Mosaics and stained-glass windows, each fabricated from thousands of pieces of tile and glass, respectively, had the effect of appearing fluid even though they were not.

◆ Chapter Four

BIBLICAL STORIES IN TILE AND GLASS

The increased size and numbers of simple parish churches and elaborate grand cathedrals created interiors in need of new and different forms of art. To meet the twin purposes of decorating interiors and educating illiterate worshippers with pictorial depictions of Christian stories, many artists preferred to work with mosaics and stained glass instead of sculptures and paintings. These four visual forms of storytelling were each referred to as the *Biblia Pauperum*, a Latin term that meant "Bible of the Poor" and alluded to the high correlation between illiteracy and poverty.

Medieval artists borrowed heavily from their Roman predecessors. Roman artisans learned by trial and error how to create glass that was translucent for use as plates and goblets. They also created colored paints called glazes that they applied to thumbnail-sized tiles called tesserae. Thousands of different-colored tesserae proved to be the perfect medium for creating designs and pictures on the floors of private Roman homes and in the pools of public baths. Whereas the Romans used mosaics exclusively for floors, however, medieval mosaicists principally applied them to church walls and domes.

The Art of Early Christian Mosaics

Early Christians were eager to build on the Roman tradition of superbly executed mosaics. Although ceramic tesserae were the dominant medium for mosaics, medieval craftsmen on occasion added small stones, bits of colored glass, and on a few rare occasions, even precious jewels and gold leaf.

Creating large-scale works covering thousands of square feet required dozens

of workers who performed several distinct jobs. Medieval mosaicists began by hauling wagonloads of clay from local riverbanks to make the tesserae. Clay was carefully selected for qualities that made it soft and smooth, able to absorb glazes, and able to dry uniformly in hot ovens called kilns without cracking or warping. Clumps of wet clay were rolled into large slabs to a uniform thickness of between 0.5 and 0.75 inches (1.25 and 2cm). While still wet, the soft slabs were cut into individual tesserae with long, taut pieces of thread that sliced them as small as 0.25 square inches (1.6 sq. cm) or as large as 1 square inch (6.5 sq. cm) depending upon the need.

The sliced slabs were then set in the kilns, where they remained for several hours while all moisture evaporated and the clay hardened. After cooling, the tesserae were painted with one of a variety of colored glazes and fired a second time to bring the colors to brilliant hues. After a final cooling, the finished rock-hard tesserae were sent to the worksite for setting.

Setters awaiting the tesserae applied final coats of stucco to the wall or ceiling that would receive the finished tiles. Artists then sketched the outlines of the mosaic with charcoal, delineating the major features and noting the colors. When the tesserae arrived, workmen

This detailed mosaic found in Venice's San Marco Cathedral depicts Noah building the ark, a well-known story from the Old Testament.

mixed smooth concrete that would bond the tesserae to the stucco. Applying thin layers of concrete to small areas at a time, workers set the tesserae and allowed them to dry. When the entire mosaic was completed, a single neutral color of concrete called grout was spread over the work to fill in the small spaces between the tesserae. Before the grout completely dried to its hardened state, workers using damp sponges wiped off the top layer of grout to expose the brilliant colors and reveal the finished mosaic.

Mosaics first became a popular art form in the churches of the Byzantine Empire, most prominently in the great cathedrals of Constantinople, but their popularity soon traveled to parts of western Europe, especially Italy. At some time during the late tenth century, Pope Leo of Ostia provided the following account of the arrival of mosaics in the Abbey of Monte Cassino, 80 miles (130km) south of Rome:

Meanwhile [Desiderius] sent envoys to Constantinople to hire artists who were experts in the art of laying mosaics. They were to decorate the apse, the arch, and the vestibule of the main basilica. The degree of perfection which was attained in these arts by the masters whom Desiderius had hired can be seen in their works. One would believe that the figures in the mosaics were alive and that flowers of every color bloomed in wonderful variety. The abbot in his wisdom decided that a great number of young monks in

The ceiling and arches of a cathedral in Palermo, Italy, are decorated with splendid and intricately detailed mosaics.

the monastery should be thoroughly initiated in these arts in order that their knowledge might not again be lost in Italy.[27]

Monte Cassino became a center for mosaics, but by no means the greatest one. That distinction belongs to the city of Ravenna on Italy's northern Adriatic coast. In several monasteries there, hundreds of millions of tesserae depict biblical stories and Christian themes.

The Regal Mosaics of Ravenna

Ravenna's unparalleled collection of mosaics is the result of its location. It was chosen as the capital of the Western Empire in 402 because it was an Adriatic port that served as a commercial, political, and cultural link between the Byzantine and the Roman cultures. Across that link, from east to west, flowed many cultural attributes of the Byzantine Empire.

For three centuries, Ravenna was the recipient of many forms of art, but the one that flourished more than all others was the making of mosaics. Once the Christian Church established its supremacy in Ravenna, it constructed a variety of edifices to serve its needs. Resplendent with mosaics are the mausoleum of Galla Placidia, a Roman empress who was a devout Christian; the churches of Saint Apollinare and Saint Apollinare Nuovo; and the most stunning of all in mosaic richness, the Church of San Vitale.

Mosaicists incorporated entire church interiors into their compositions. All architectural features could be covered in mosaics: walls, apses, cupolas, arches, vaults, and niches. By covering all interior spaces, both vertical and horizontal, foreground and background, a single work might occupy spaces on different planes. Thus, mosaics could convey a look of three-dimensionality that escaped fresco painters of the time.

Mosaicists also excelled in adding visual effects that painters never achieved. By inserting tesserae made from a variety of reflective materials, they created sparkles of light on highlighted areas of a mosaic. In early Romanesque churches that relied almost exclusively on candles for interior illumination, the flickering candlelight was beautifully reflected off curved domes covered in tesserae, bits of glass, and gold leaf.

The Apse of Saint Apollinare

One of the mosaics that brought fame to Ravenna was the immense mosaic that covered the domed apse of Saint Apollinare, a work that is widely considered by art historians to be one of the finest masterpieces of mosaic art. The subject

The Church of San Vitale in Ravenna, the capital of the Western Roman Empire, houses some of the most magnificent mosaics in the world.

expressed in the apse was the Transfiguration of Christ, a holy moment in the Christian tradition. According to the New Testament, Jesus led his apostles Peter, James, and John to pray at the top of a mountain. There, Jesus suddenly became transfigured when his face shone like the sun and his clothes turned brilliant white. Two Old Testament prophets, Elijah and Moses, then spoke with Jesus as a bright cloud appeared overhead, and the voice of God proclaimed from the cloud, "This is my Son, the Beloved. Listen to him." Many churches had representations of the Transfiguration of Christ, but few if any were more respected than this one. In the opinion of art historians writing for an Italian art Web site, this church "is occupied by one of the most splendid (if not the most splendid) theophany [appearance of God] of Christian antiquity: the great symbolic transfiguration."[28]

The creators of this great mosaic employed clever symbolism to tell the story of the Transfiguration. The largest symbol, dead center in the apse, is the cross, which symbolizes Jesus's death as a sacrifice for all humanity. Immediately above it is a hand extending down from a misty swirl to represent the presence of God in the cloud. To the left and right of the cross, depicted within a wavelike swirl of tesserae, are the two prophets Moses and Elijah, respectively. Immediately below the prophets are three sheep representing the apostles with whom Christ went to pray. In the center, below the sheep, stands Saint Apollinare, and to his left and right are groves of palm trees

symbolizing the eternal life Christ promised for all who followed his teachings. To the left and right of the feet of Apollinare is a flock of sheep representing the church's congregation.

The drama of the work was further heightened by the use of gold leaf, enamel, and glass tesserae interspaced among the ceramic ones. Candlelight reflected off the mosaic in such a way to recall the flashes of light associated with the biblical transformation story.

The interplay of candlelight and tesserae prompted some architects to experiment with the effects of sunlight for illuminating interiors. Those designing the grand Gothic cathedrals, especially in France, England, and Germany, created great banks of colored glass windows that surpassed in color and drama the stories told in mosaics.

Divine Light for Gothic Interiors

Long before the first hues of blue and red light from stained-glass windows fell across church floors, light had served as a spiritual metaphor. Light was embraced by theologians as a symbol for truth, wisdom, and honesty. Darkness, on the other hand, symbolized the forces of hell typified by lying, deception, and sin. To conquer the forces of darkness, builders of Gothic cathedrals flooded their interiors with cleansing heavenly light. In the opinion of Friedrich Heer, author of *The Fires of Faith*, "The magnificence, which transformed the cathedral of the thirteenth

Manufacturing Gold Leaf

The gold leaf used on Byzantine icons and illuminated manuscripts consisted of very thin sheets, or leaves, of pure gold. Its use was desired because of the way it highlighted parts of a decorative scene by reflecting light that caught the attention of the viewer. According to Christopher De Hamel in his book *Medieval Craftsmen: Scribes and Illuminators*, the fourteenth-century craftsman Cennino Cennini stated in one of his writings that "goldbeaters could make 145 leaves of gold from hammering one ducat [an Italian coin]." Each ducat weighed 0.12 ounces (3.5 grams), and although Cennini does not specify the size of the leaves, scholars estimate that one ducat, properly beaten, could yield about 30 square feet (2.8 sq. m) of leaf. Knowing when to stop beating was a matter of experience. Cennini advises gold beaters to "examine the gold often and if you find it rippling and matt, like goat parchment, then consider it good." Since gold leaf was used sparingly, more than 1 square foot (0.1 sq. m) for an icon or entire book would have been considered lavish.

The character of gold is such that regardless of thinness, it never cracks, tears, or crumbles. Scholars have measured gold leaf from medieval art and discovered it to be as thin as 1/10,000 of a millimeter. Monks and artists who beat gold coins with flat-head hammers learned that the thinner the leaf, the more easily it could be shaped and applied to works of art. According to De Hamel, artists observed that "if rubbed between the fingers and thumb, it will fade to nothing, if dropped it hardly seems to flutter downwards, if wrinkled, it can be straightened out with a puff of breath, and if eaten, it seems to vanish on the tongue."

Gold leaf, incredibly thin sheets of pure gold, was used to accentuate this fresco found in an Italian cathedral.

How Glass Was Made During the Middle Ages

Workers mixed sand, salt, and ash together, melting them over a wood fire. Next they sometimes added different kinds of powdered metals to the molten mixture to color the glass.

The glassmakers then dipped a large hollow rod into the molten glass, forming a large bubble by blowing into the rod.

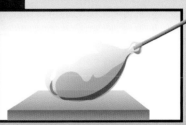

This bubble was cut open at the end and spun into a huge disk. If the glass was not colored at this point, powdered metals could be sprinkled over the still-hot glass to create brilliant hues.

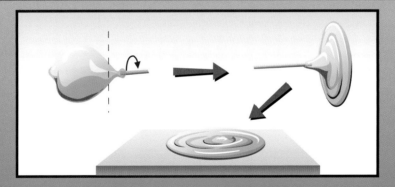

Molten glass could also be blown into a tube shape, then slit along the side and flattened into a sheet of glass.

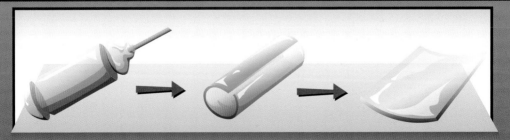

century into a forerunner of the heavenly city, had its most obvious manifestation in the glory of its stained glass windows."[29]

Credit for the sudden demand for colored glass that arose in the early twelfth century with the first Gothic cathedrals belongs to Abbot Suger of the abbey at Saint-Denis near Paris. Suger believed an architectural style that drenched worshipers in light would make them feel more uplifted and closer to God than the dark and somber Romanesque style that had gone before. Suger once commented, "Best of all things, most delectable, most beautiful is natural light; it is divine light that constitutes the perfection and beauty of all material forms."[30]

Suger's commitment to stained glass created an industry of craftsmen who produced it. In miserable heat, local glazers wearing leather aprons transferred molten glass from hot ovens with long iron tongs, carefully rolled it into flat sheets, and then passed it on to others who added the rich colors. These local glazers took pride in the beauty they created, unlike the migrant bands of glazers who roamed from town to town. For them, creating stained glass was nothing more than a job that paid for their room and meals. Nonetheless, their work was considered divine by those who worshipped in the radiance of their colored windows. Modern art historians, such as H.W. Janson, praise medieval glaziers because "the 'miraculous' light that floods the choir through the 'most sacred' windows becomes the Light Divine, a mystic revelation of the spirit of God."[31]

Parishioners in each major city in Europe took special pride in the stained glass of their local cathedral. Each cathedral had its unique glass designs, but few architects dared dispute that the glass displays in the Church of Sainte-Chapelle in Paris brightened that cathedral with greater intensity than any other.

Sainte-Chapelle de Paris

The history of this church begins in 1239, when King Louis IX of France acquired what he believed to be the crown of thorns that had been placed on Christ's head as he was led to his death and a piece of the cross on which he was crucified. Those two acquisitions were so holy that Louis ordered the construction of a major cathedral to house and honor them. The result was the Gothic cathedral of Sainte-Chapelle in Paris. By the time the cathedral was completed in 1248, the fame of its stained glass windows overshadowed that of its relics.

The size of Sainte-Chapelle is relatively modest compared to its much larger companion cathedral, Notre Dame, just a few blocks away. Yet, with interior dimensions of just 118 feet (36m) long, 56 feet (17m) wide, and 70 feet (21m) high, it nonetheless contains the greatest proportion of stained glass to stone wall space of any Gothic cathedral. Bathed in the reflection of exquisite blues, greens, yellows, and reds, the vaulted stone ceiling appears to float above fifteen banks of magnificent stained-glass windows

Coloring Stained Glass

The skills needed to create stained glass were developed during the early twelfth century and raised to a high art form a century later. Colored stained glass was not actually stained, which is a process of applying colors on the surface of clear glass and allowing them to adhere to the surface. During the Middle Ages, color was added to the glass when it was in a molten state so that the color permeated throughout the glass, not just on the surface.

The first step in the stained-glass process was the production of the clear glass. The glass was made with a formula of sand, salt, and tree ashes. These three ingredients were heated in furnaces fueled by wood until they melted into a thick, molten mass.

The hot, viscous glass was removed from the furnace and placed on an iron table, where it was allowed to spread out. At

Glassmakers created the vivid hues found in stained glass by using such materials as powdered minerals, vegetables, and sugar.

this point, the colors that gave the glass its brilliant hues were created by sprinkling over the liquid glass a variety of chemicals. Workers added powdered cobalt for blues, copper for reds, sulfur for yellows, nickel for grays, and malachite for green.

On occasion yams or turnips were sprinkled into the molten glass to impart a murky, uneven appearance. Workers even added sugar, which, when melted, gave the glass an amber tint. Different hues were the result of mixing several chemicals. Through trial and error, medieval glassmakers learned how to produce a wide range of colors.

that are collectively called the clerestory. The clerestory occupies 6,500 square feet (600 sq. m) of space. Each bank is so tall, 40 feet (12m), yet narrow at 11 feet (3.3m), that stone vertical supports between each

bank were necessary to prevent the collapse of the walls.

On a sunny day, the interior of the chapel is ablaze with light from these windows. In Sainte-Chapelle's fifteen panels, biblical stories are recounted in 1,134 different images that surround the interior down both sides and around the front of the church. Hundreds of thousands of individual pieces of glass, secured in place by lead frames, tell the major Old Testament stories of the creation of the world, Adam and Eve, Noah's Ark, and Moses delivering the Ten Commandments. Hundreds of thousands more illustrate the New Testament stories about the life of Jesus, including those of his birth, baptism by John the Baptist, crucifixion, and resurrection. Among the depictions of the major stories of the Bible, dozens of glass portraits of significant Christian figures are interspersed.

Today, two-thirds of the original glass remains in place. Wars, riots during the French Revolution of 1789, and sporadic vandalism have claimed the other third. During the nineteenth century, all of the glass was removed for cleaning and restoration, and it was removed again for safekeeping during World War II in anticipation of the German invasion of Paris. Following the war, every piece was meticulously replaced.

Clerestories like that of Sainte-Chapelle, which radiated polychromatic light into chapel interiors, gradually gave way to a more dominant and spectacular form of

Sainte-Chapelle Cathedral in Paris, famous for its many magnificent stained-glass windows, has proportionately more stained glass than any other Gothic cathedral.

window called the rose. Circular rather than rectangular, and held in place by stone latticework called tracery rather than lead, rose windows gradually emerged as the pinnacle of stained-glass compositions.

Great Rose Windows

Rose windows took their name from their resemblance to an unfolding rosebud. In keeping with the gigantic Gothic cathedrals of the time, these exotic works of art were enormous—33 feet (10m) in diameter for the two at Notre Dame Cathedral in Paris and 43 feet (13m) for

the one at Notre Dame in Chartres. Rose windows served several purposes, as historian Eldred Aelfwald explains:

The rose window operates on many levels: spiritual, meditative, and emotional. Abbot Suger's observations underscore how deep an emotional and spiritual chord is struck by the play of light that passes through the glass. The instructional aspect of rose windows is plainly visible by the subjects chosen for display in each petal.... Simply following the tracery with the eye and taking in the patterns found in a

Secrets of Cooking and Cutting Glass

The furnaces for making glass were large, rectangular kilns, some having a hot surface of up to 100 square feet (9.3 sq. m) or more. They were made of three to four layers of stone and clay about 4 feet (1.2m) high with arched ceilings for placing and removing the pots of bubbling glass. The bottom layer contained the furnace, where beech wood, the most common hardwood, was burned. Later, the wood ash was mixed with sand, turning it into a thick muck that was placed near the furnace, where it cooled very slowly to prevent brittleness.

After another period of simmering, the glass was blown into a large glob by

a worker using a thin iron blowpipe. Another worker called the gaffer then took the glob, reheated it, and placed it on a flat table until it was smooth and nearing a hard consistency. The next worker, called the slitter, sliced the flattened sheet of glass on a wooden platform using a hot flatiron. Then, the individual pieces of glass needed by the designer were cut from the sheets. In times before hard diamond-tipped cutters were available, workers cut the needed pieces by tracing the line of cut with urine or spit. This technique prevented the glass from shattering.

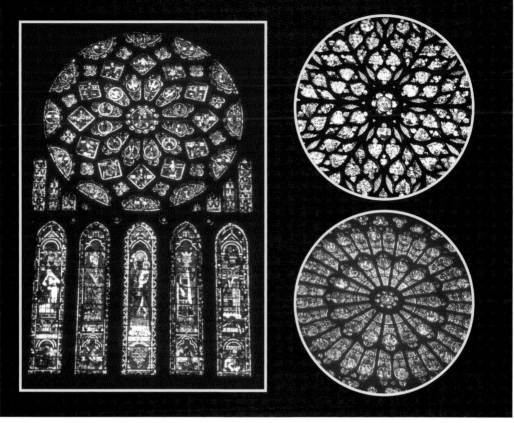

The rose window, depicting scenes from the life of Christ and other biblical scenes, was the centerpiece of the exterior of the medieval cathedral. Three dazzling examples are pictured.

rose window can put one into a very calm or meditative mood."[32]

The principal subject of the great roses is the Virgin and Child, but others include major events from the life of Christ. In all cases, the center portion of the rose, called the rosette, was reserved for the main subject. On the outer regions of the rose, known as the petals, other biblical scenes were arranged.

Containing these enormous displays that consisted of hundreds of thousands of individual pieces of glass and weighed several tons was a remarkable engineer-ing feat. The span and weight of each rose necessitated stone tracery to support them. The tracery was carved by sculptors who worked closely with the glassmakers to ensure it perfectly conformed to each panel and provided sufficient strength to hold the work in place.

Great rose windows and colorful clerestories were dramatic works of cathedral art, but other more modest ones were also prominently displayed. During the celebration of the Mass each Sunday, a variety of small, practical art forms created by local craftspeople also played major roles.

Biblical Stories in Tile and Glass 63

Chapter Five

ART TO CELEBRATE THE MASS

Celebrating the Mass was the principal activity required of most medieval Europeans each Sunday. Each Mass consisted of a series of well-coordinated rites, prayers, and ceremonies culminating in the high point, the taking of Communion, formally called the Eucharist. Wherever people attended Mass throughout western Europe, they could count on a high degree of commonality in the event, its sequence, and the Latin language in which it was conducted.

The Mass was both serious and dramatic. It involved the use of relics and other objects required by tradition. Initially simple and practical, each piece within the collection of paraphernalia was gradually raised to an art form with the advent of elaborate Gothic architecture and its accompanying art. This reflected the belief of Church authorities that each part of the church and

church service should be of similar quality and artistic value.

The parish churches and major cathedrals that peppered Europe spawned small cottage businesses that crafted the items used each Sunday. Local craftspeople specializing in wood, metal, ivory, paints, and textiles provided all of the needed accessories. In the process, and over time, artisans added embellishments, changed designs, and incorporated local artistic variations that added unique regional touches to their creations.

The predictability of all Sunday Masses included the sequence of events. The moment worshippers stepped through the main portal of the church or cathedral, they knew what was about to occur.

This thirteenth-century Italian crucifixion scene poignantly captures the sufferings and death of Jesus on the cross.

The Crucifix

Entering a church typically brought parishioners into the nave, where their first focus of attention was meant to be on a crucifix, a representation of Jesus's death on the cross. No Christian symbol had greater power over a congregation's emotions than that of Jesus suffering and dying on the cross. Every church in Christendom, regardless of size or simplicity, prominently placed a crucifix to remind the congregation of Christ's sacrifice.

Size, quality of craftsmanship, and level of sophistication were unique to each crucifix. Early wood examples that exist from the tenth century were little more than two pieces of wood nailed together with a rudimentary carving of Christ executed by an untrained sculptor. By the thirteenth century, however, as Gothic cathedrals spread across the European landscape, crucifixes grew in size and became more elaborate, dramatic, and colorful.

Several examples of early-thirteenth-century ornate crucifixes can still be seen today. In most examples, Christ wears only a simple loincloth and looks out toward the viewer. Appearing calm in spite of his tragic condition, he slumps slightly to one side with either no blood or only a few drops flowing from the four nails driven through his hands and feet. Small panels under the horizontal crosspiece, one each to the left and right of his body, depict scenes of the grief that his followers experienced as he died. These crucifixes are collectively called the *Christus Triumphans.* Latin for "Triumphant Christ," because in the words of art historian Stephanie Brown, they are "essentially triumphant images. They present an awe-inspiring God, a phoenix-like figure, the survivor of death."[33]

During the fourteenth and fifteenth centuries, the *Christus Triumphans* was replaced by the *Christus Patiens,* the Suffering Christ. No longer stoical, Christ is portrayed in these works as a man suffering an agonizing and painful death. This suffering is expressed by his contorted body, drooping head, and closed eyes. The violent nature of his death is emphasized by volumes of blood that flow from his nail wounds. Many of these representations also show the crown of thorns on his head, blood dripping down his face, and a deep gash in his side where a Roman soldier was said to have lanced him as he hung on the cross.

The increasingly grisly depictions reflected changing attitudes toward Christ. Art historians explain that the intensity of the horror was intended to remind parishioners that Christ had sacrificed himself for their redemption so that they might enter the kingdom of heaven. The more horrific his crucifixion appeared to be, the thinking went, the more seriously the faithful would adhere to the teachings of the Church. In the opinion of art historian Ellen Ross, writing in her book, *The Grief of God:* "For the medieval Christians, the blood flowing from the wounds of Jesus Christ is the love of God literally poured out onto all of humankind. Divine compassion rains down upon humanity in the shedding of Jesus Christ's blood, and viewers are invited to enter into the joy . . . through the bloody wounds of Jesus' flesh."[34]

As worshippers reflected on the meaning of the crucifix while proceeding to their pews, they walked toward the altar, which was set on the floor at the far end of the church. Intended to be large and dominant, it was the place where the most important rites of the Mass took place.

The Altar

The altar provided a focal point for the Mass. The priest or bishop used it as a table to hold all of the objects used during the service, including candles, the Bible, and specially designed vessels that held the bread and wine consumed during the Eucharist.

Altars, like crucifixes, ran the gamut of sizes, shapes, and level of embellishment. Wood was the most common material used for the altar, but a few examples made of marble are known, as well as even rarer ones with ivory panels. One document dating from 812 included an inventory of a church that had this entry: "We found in the [German] island called Staffelsee a church built in honor of St. Michael, within which was an altar finished in gold and silver."[35]

Regardless of the material from which the altar was made, the side visible to the congregation was typically carved with religious scenes. The most common was the Last Supper because the Eucharist, which was celebrated at the altar, commemorates that significant event. A vari-

The main altar in a German cathedral depicts the apostles standing at the base of the cross as Jesus is crucified.

ety of Christian symbols was also commonly included, such as the alpha-omega sign, which represents the birth and death of Christ; a triangle representing the Holy Trinity of God, Christ, and the Holy Ghost; and sometimes a downward-swooping dove symbolizing the presence of the Holy Ghost.

Once the faithful were seated, all heads turned to observe the processional as it entered and proceeded down the nave to the altar. Members of the processional included the acolytes, who lit the altar candles and assisted in other rituals; the deacon, who acted as the steward of church monies collected during the Mass; the priest; and on special occasions, the

local bishop. As the members of the processional moved forward, their official robes, called vestments, created an impressive and somber spectacle.

Vestments

The requirement that vestments be worn during the Mass can be found in the Old Testament book of Exodus. It says: "You must make sacred vestments for your brother Aaron to consecrate him to serve as priest to me. The following are the vestments you must make: a pouch or breast piece, an apron, a robe, a brocaded tunic, a mitre and a girdle, and they must use gold, violet, purple, and scarlet yarn and fine linen."[36]

By the eleventh century, vestments came to reflect a person's status in the Church hierarchy. Particular attention was paid to the vestments of the bishops to make them distinct from those of the priests. From that time forward, bishops when fully vested wore a camisia or shirt, a neck cloth or amice, a long white undergarment called an alb, a tunic called a dalmatic, a stole, and a chasuble—a long, ornate outer garment. Of these, the most elaborate and indicative of the rank of bishop was the chasuble.

The chasuble was typically made in a local woolen mill. Similar to an immense cloak, it was sewn in such a way that the only opening was a hole for the head. According to a few medieval records, a single chasuble that hung from the shoulders, over both arms, and down to the feet required the wool of two sheep.

To create the effect of grandeur, ornate designs were sewn onto the fabric of the chasuble. These varied from region to region, but colorful floral designs were popular for the back and a crucifix frequently appeared on the front. Chasubles of different colors were worn depending upon the ceremony: black for funerals, white for Easter and Christmas, red for Good Friday, and green for most Sundays.

Chasubles for major celebrations were often made of finer materials than everyday ones. Favored were silk fabrics imported from Constantinople. During the late Middle Ages, sumptuous silk brocades with flowers, fruits, and small forest animals were increasingly common. Some chasubles even had precious stones incorporated into the design along the hem and sleeve cuffs.

As the bishop moved up the nave in his ornate chasuble, his high rank was further emphasized to the congregation by the elaborate staff he carried, called a crosier. This staff was used as a walking stick and was also a symbol of authority. The association of the crosier with bishops caused it to be commonly called the "bishop's staff."

Pictured is an embroidered chasuble that belonged to the thirteenth-century pope Benedict XI.

The Crosier

As key figures in the Church, bishops were responsible for the spiritual welfare of all people within their regions. In this capacity, they held spiritual, political, and administrative roles exceeded only by a handful of archbishops and the pope. Since bishops thus served as symbolic shepherds of their flocks, the crosier each carried was modeled after a shepherd's crook. The crosier also symbolically linked the holder with Christ, who was often referred to as a shepherd to his flock of believers.

Each bishop's crosier was made individually in accordance with his preferences. Most bishops expected the staff to exceed their height by about 6 inches (15 cm). The crosier was usually heavily decorated. A typical one was ornamented with bands of gold inlay on the shaft and leaves along the curved portion in keeping with Roman designs used on column capitals. More elaborate designs were also crafted. One crosier that has survived includes a defiant eagle that clutches the Bible in one claw. Flecks of paint on the bird indicate that the crosier was at one time polychrome and covered with gold leaf. A second example, this one from Limerick, Ireland, has an inscription dated 1418 and notes that its craftsman was Thomas O'Carryd. He lavishly decorated the crosier with a spiraling row of gold figures that include Saint Patrick and Saint Munchin, both patron saints of Limerick and Ireland.

Diptychs and Triptychs

Once the bishop and his entourage reached the altar, the acolytes lit the candles and opened diptychs and triptychs—two- and three-panel decorative sculptured art objects that were shaped like books and placed on the altar. These works had hinges that allowed them to be opened and closed. Each panel contained a sculpted or carved scene. The most embellished and rarest examples were carved from ivory, but other versions were made of sculpted bronze panels with embedded gems.

The purpose of diptychs and triptychs was the same as other art forms—to remind worshippers of familiar biblical stories. Their unique quality was their hinged sculptured form. The hinged panels protected the valuable art inside when closed, yet provided for dramatic display when opened. In triptychs, side panels were hinged to an unmoving central panel and swung out when open and in when closed. Churches often owned a variety of triptychs, each of which was associated with a different important Christian holy day such as Easter or Christmas. During important celebrations, the appropriate diptychs or triptychs were brought forth and displayed on the altar. The rest of the year, they remained closed in safe storage.

Diptychs and triptychs were also favored religious objects taken on long journeys by priests as well as parishioners. Their hinged construction meant that two or three icons could be conveniently folded up and safely packed away for use during evening and morning prayers. Not only were diptychs and triptychs portable, many were also lockable.

The most common theme represented in triptychs was the Passion of Christ. The central panel generally depicted Christ on the cross, with two soldiers standing nearby with a sheet in which they will wrap his body. In the background is often a group of weeping women. The left-hand panel usually depicts the apostle Peter denying that he knows Christ just before the crucifixion, and the right panel shows Judas throwing away the money he was paid to betray Christ.

Once the acolytes had opened the diptychs and triptychs, prayers were said and preparation was made for the Eucharist, the high point of the Mass. This was the one time that the bishop and priest directly interacted with the congregation, offering them wine and bread from sacred vessels.

Sacred Vessels

One of the highest art forms created by silversmiths and goldsmiths were the vessels used during the Eucharist. According to tradition, the Communion represents Christ's Last Supper, at which time he passed a cup of wine and plate of bread to each of his twelve apostles and told

Triptychs, three-panel sculptured art objects, were unfolded on the altar in order to illustrate biblical stories during worship services.

Relics as Art

One common activity of medieval Christians was to gaze upon and pray before venerated relics. These consisted of physical remains believed to be from holy persons, such as bones, hair, and teeth; or objects associated with Christ. Churches were built to house these relics and honor these holy persons' contributions to Christianity.

Relics were enclosed in lavish containers visible to the faithful through glass windows. Known as reliquaries, these containers were often boxes made of intricately carved rare woods, glass and bronze cabinets, or jewel-encrusted containers. The design of the reliquary, and carvings on it, communicated to the viewer the history of the relic and its Christian significance. Because famous reliquaries sometimes attracted more visitors than did the church in which they were displayed, no expense was spared in their creation.

The artistic display of reliquaries heightened their appeal. Adjacent money boxes were set up to collect donations from the faithful who might be emotionally moved by the sight of bones, the prison chains of martyrs, or hair. Relics were typically stored in an underground vault during the night and placed on display each morning for public viewing. Enclosed in crimson silk or velvet curtains, the containers were ceremoniously escorted to their places for viewing and locked in place.

This medieval bust of Saint Permerina doubles as a reliquary.

them to partake of the wine, which represented his blood, and the bread, which represented his body. During the Eucharist, it was believed that the priest or bishop transformed the wine and bread into the blood and body of Christ, a conversion called transubstantiation. Because of this transformation, special care was given to the proper performance of the ritual as well as the vessels that were used.

The two most important vessels were the chalice, which contained the wine, and the ciborium, which held pieces of bread. In small, rural, medieval churches, the chalice and ciborium might have been simple cups made of pewter, alabaster, silver, or even wood. The chalices of the great cathedrals, however, became increasingly ornate as the Middle Ages progressed. To the bishops and archbishops of Canterbury, Paris, Florence, Basel, Nuremberg, and Athens, the wine and bread could touch only gold, the most precious metal known at the time. The exteriors of these gold vessels were often decorated with precious gems and pearls.

The elaborate ornamentation of the chalice and ciborium did not seem excessive or garish to the faithful. Abbot Suger, for example, believed that one of his duties was to embellish Saint-Denis Cathedral by all means possible for the glory of God. He made this point very clear in discussing the significance of the vessels used during the Eucharist:

Personally I deem it right and proper that all that is most valuable should be employed, exclusively, to celebrate the holy Eucharist. If golden pouring vessels were used, according to the word of God to collect the blood of goats and calves and red heifers [references to the Bible], how much more must

golden vessels, precious stones, and whatever is most valued among created things, be laid out with continual reference and full devotion for the reception of the blood of Christ![37]

Following the Eucharist, the Mass ended with the exit of the processional. On occasion, however, when a baptism was planned, this rite of symbolically cleansing away original sin was performed

This ornately decorated Byzantine chalice features enamel representations of Jesus and the apostles.

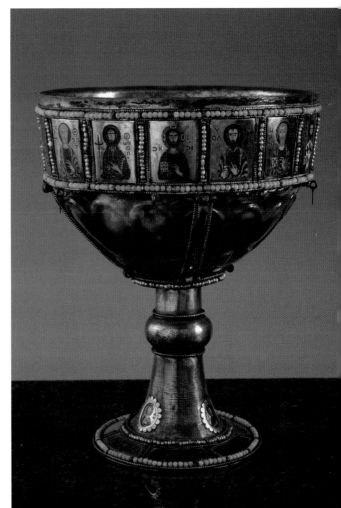

A Critic of Christian Art

The flurry of Christian art was not embraced by all high-ranking clerics. Exquisite sculptures, paintings, and objects used to perform the Mass were opposed by a handful of influential Church leaders who believed such art forms were distractions for those who came to Mass for prayer.

One of the harshest critics was the early-twelfth-century monk Bernard, Abbot of Clairvaux, France. He thought that artistic embellishments were inappropriate for a strict religious lifestyle. Bernard believed that worshippers should attend Mass without being surrounded by needlessly luxurious objects. Furthermore, he protested what he believed to be the needless expense of art. The following excerpt from his scathing criticism of religious art is from his treatise, Apologia to Abbot William, *found in Leslie Ross's book,* Artists of the Middle Ages:

I shall say nothing about the soaring heights and extravagant lengths and unnecessary widths of the churches, nothing about their expensive decorations and their novel images, which catch the attention of those who go in to pray, and dry up their devotion. . . . Oh vanity of vanities, whose vanity is rivaled only by its insanity! The walls of the church are aglow, but the poor of the church go hungry. The stones of the church are covered with gold, while its children are left naked. The food of the poor is taken to feed the eyes of the rich, and amusement is provided for the curious, while the needy have not even the necessities of life. . . . One could spend the whole day gazing fascinated at these things, one by one, instead of meditating on the law of God. Good Lord, even if the foolishness of it all occasions no shame, at least one might balk at the expense.

at the baptismal font immediately following the Eucharist.

Baptismal Fonts

Two types of baptisms were performed during the Middle Ages. One was full-body immersion, believed to be the method used by John the Baptist to baptize Jesus in the Jordan River, and the other anointment, or the splashing of a small amount of water on the subject's head. Immersing adults required a large pool built either into the floor of the church, far to one side of the altar, or more commonly in a separate building called a baptistery. At a later time, when child baptism became preferred over adult baptism, babies were anointed with water from a small, movable font placed close to the altar, in full view of the congregation.

Baptismal fonts, like all other forms of medieval religious art, could be simple and plain or sophisticated and highly decorated. Whether the font was made of coarse stone, polished marble, or bronze, its base was always octagonal because the number eight was associated with the resurrection of Christ, which occurred eight days after he had entered Jerusalem. The most requested decoration carved or painted on the side of the bowl-shaped font was the baptism of Christ. What made this particular depiction unique was the way sculptors rendered the two men in the river. The water below their waists was shown as wavy lines that suggested ripples, and their legs were carved only roughly to suggest murkiness.

Following the baptism, candles were extinguished, diptychs and triptychs closed, and a final prayer was recited. The entourage of church leaders and acolytes then exited the church with as much solemnity and pageantry as when they had entered. Once the congregation exited the church, few had need of any further spiritual guidance until the next Sunday.

Churches and cathedrals throughout Europe provided parishioners with all they needed to reflect properly on the glory of God. These edifices, however, which primarily functioned as places of prayer and secondarily as museums of religious art, could not assist the faithful during private prayer or while they were traveling and far from a church. To help them, two classes of artists known as scribes and illuminators emerged to create elaborately painted prayers in the form of books and manuscripts.

Chapter Six

PAINTED PRAYERS

Before the invention of mechanical printing presses, books were hand-made objects—technically referred to as manuscripts—valued as works of art and as repositories of eternal knowledge. Expensive and unable to be read by the illiterate poor, Bibles and prayer books, unlike the visual arts within the church, were exclusively within the reach of monks, priests, and rich families.

During the Middle Ages, the Bible was considered a sacred object that functioned as a spiritual conduit between readers and God and the saints. In the opinion of Roger S. Wieck in his book, *Painted Prayers: The Book of Hours in Medieval and Renaissance Art,* "At a time when the laity's access to God was very much controlled and limited by others than themselves, books bestowed direct, democratic, and potentially uninterrupted access to God, the Virgin Mary, and the saints."[38]

Making a book of several hundred pages by hand was a monumental undertaking. Each step in the creation of a manuscript required intensive labor. Sometimes these projects involved the collaboration of entire workshops. At a time before the invention of paper, pages were made from vellum, cut to size, and sewn into sections called quires. Inks had to be mixed; quills prepared from large, high-quality feathers; and the pages ruled for lettering. Copyists, known as scribes, labored in workshops called scriptoria, duplicating the text from an existing manuscript to a new one. On occasion artists might embellish manuscripts with illustrations, known as illuminations, such as decorative initials and ornaments in the margins. The most lavish medieval manuscripts, when completed, were bound in thick leather covers set with jewels.

Most scribes during the Middle Ages were monks living in monasteries. During the early years of the Middle Ages, prayer and copying manuscripts were their way of fulfilling their obligation of *orare et laborare.*

Copying Early Bibles

With the collapse of the Western Roman Empire came the collapse of what had been a flourishing manuscript trade. For a thousand years prior to that event, wealthy educated Greeks and Romans had amassed personal libraries of manuscripts representing the greatest thinkers such as Aeschylus, Sophocles, Aristotle, Socrates, and Homer. But with the end of the Roman Empire and the beginning of the chaotic Middle Ages, entire libraries of rare manuscripts began to disappear.

What saved the vanishing literary tradition of Europe was the rise of monasteries. Monks were required to listen to biblical readings during meals and in chapel and to read silently in their rooms by candlelight. Readings included the works of philosophers and theologians, the Bible, and prayer books, and monks in some monasteries were required to read at least one book each year in addition to the Bible. The requirement to read gradually encouraged the copying of manuscripts to increase their availability. The personal ownership of books was forbidden, so each monastery built a library to house a communal set of manuscripts.

The copying of manuscripts was a job perfectly suited for monks who pursued silent and prayerful lives apart from the rest of Europeans. Each scriptorium had a director to oversee the selection of manuscripts to be copied and the quality of

An illustration from the thirteenth century depicts monks working intently at their desks as they copy manuscripts.

Crafting Quills

Each scribe selected and prepared his own quills. Drawings from the Middle Ages indicate that each scribe kept dozens at hand. The best and strongest quills were those taken from living birds during the spring when they had just molted and replaced all of their feathers. The very finest were made from the five outer feathers from the left wing. The left wing was favored because the feathers curved outward and away when used by the right-handed scribes. The most sought-after feathers were those from the swan because they held their tip the longest and their hollow shaft held the most ink.

The scribe prepared the quill by paring away the tip on each side with his penknife and then slitting it up the center. Finally the point of the quill was given one final cut to create a squared-off tip. The tip spread with use and had to be recut often in the course of copying a manuscript. It is estimated that a scribe might sharpen a quill every ten or fifteen minutes or sharpen a large number of quills each morning.

the final product. The scriptorium was typically furnished with specially constructed tables where scribes sat, either on a stool or on their knees, to copy the works. Each table had a wood holder for the page being copied, a sloping desk surface for the fresh page, and a small table to hold tools. These tools included a selection of quills from swans, geese, or crows; ink pots; a small knife called a penknife for sharpening the tips of quills; and a compass used to measure the spaces between letters, words, and lines.

Sitting at his desk, each scribe generally received one large sheet of vellum at a time that he folded in half and then again to quarters to make four pages known as a quarto. He affixed a mark on each page that identified him as the scribe, determined the correct spacing and the size of the letters, and dipped his quill in the ink pot. Slowly and meticulously he copied page after page. The tip of the quill gradually spread with use, requiring the scribe to sharpen the tip with his penknife to maintain clean pen strokes. Mistakes were frequently made, and each page required a careful proofreading. If a proofreader discovered a mistake, an attempt was made to erase it with grit. If that failed, the sheet was destroyed and a new one issued.

The most commonly copied book was the Bible. Because Bibles in particular were regarded as objects that should be beautiful to reflect the importance of the messages they carried, monks by the eighth century were striving to make letters as artistically as possible. Attention to the design of individual letters became an art form called calligraphy, a term derived from two Greek words meaning "beautiful writing."

Calligraphy and Prayer

In this way, the scriptoria of monasteries, which were originally intended to be nothing more than workshops for preserving classical and Christian writings, became centers for artistic endeavors by the twelfth century. Copying the Bible and other religious documents for the purpose of spreading Church doctrine was enhanced by artistically beautifying the written word.

As calligraphy developed, increased attention was paid to both uppercase and lowercase letters and the layout of each page to create the most appealing presentation possible. Scribes practiced applying varying pressure on the tips of their quills to create thicker or thinner lines. They experimented with a variety

This detail of a capital letter "D" from an illuminated French manuscript depicts a pregnant noblewoman.

of tip shapes to produce square letters or round ones, slanted letters to the left or right, added swirls to capital letters, and even overlapped letters to create a decorative effect.

The spacing of letters and words was raised to an art form as well. Before copying, scribes used charcoal to lightly line each page vertically and horizontally at regular intervals—every quarter or half inch—to divide it into precise spaces that would each be filled with a single letter. This created a neat and easily read page. When the copying was completed and the ink dried, a light sanding of the page removed the guidelines. Each new paragraph was further enhanced by enlarging and embellishing the first letter. Such letters became known as historiated initials.

Careful, precise calligraphy could become tedious. Some scribes completed only one Bible or two or three prayer books a year, while others copied the same page day after day. Complaints were not unusual, especially in the winter when fingers became stiff and the cold caused lapses in concentration that led to misspellings. On occasion, frustrated monks added personal comments in the margins of their manuscripts. Some of the more revealing are, "Only three fingers are writing, but the whole body is suffering," "Finally it is dinner time," "The scribe has a right to the best wine," "My parchment [vellum] is the roughest in the world," and "I am not sure if the number [I am copying] is 1,000 or 10,000."[39]

Manuscripts gained in popularity when scribes experimented with decorations called illuminations. At first these artistic touches were simple, but with time they became increasingly elaborate and colorful. As illuminated manuscripts increased in popularity, an entirely different group of workers called illuminators emerged who specialized in designing pictures and applying dazzling colors.

Illuminations

Illuminated manuscripts represented the highest standard of medieval manuscripts. These specially decorated manuscripts had great value to bishops, archbishops, and popes, as well as wealthy private collectors, all of whom treasured them as high art as well as the word of God. Not surprisingly, their popularity coincided with the development of the beautiful and refined architecture and art forms of the Gothic period.

Illuminations were applied after the work of the scribes was completed. When an illuminator received a completed page from a scribe, it had blank spaces reserved for artwork and directions specifying the design, size, and colors of ink to be used. On occasion, the illumination might fill an entire page. The illuminator first prepared the area to be painted by rubbing it with a pumice stone or finely powdered glass applied with a piece of bread to create a smooth finish.

One of two methods was used to execute the design. If a monastery did not have well-trained illuminators, the pictures were copied from purchased designs. In such cases, the illuminator simply

Preparing Vellum

Vellum was generally made from sheep, pig, goat, or calf skins but on occasion, skins of smaller animals such as rabbits were used. No matter which skins were used, the process of preparing them for the calligrapher and illuminator was time-consuming and tedious.

Skins were initially soaked in a lime solution in wooden vats or in stone-lined pits. They were kept there from three to ten days, depending upon the temperature, and were occasionally stirred and turned. Finally they were washed in clean water. Each skin was then stretched on a wood frame, and both sides were scraped of any remaining hairs or skin tissue with a strigil, a curved, blunt-edged knife. Some medieval instructions stated that the skin should be scraped when wet; others stated that it should be scraped when dry. When the skin was dry and it had been scraped, it was again wetted with either water or beer and then pounced, or rubbed with pumice. Pouncing smoothed the surface and removed blemishes. The skin was then completely rewetted and dried again under tension. Finally it was finished by a second pouncing, and perhaps by rubbing chalk or some other compound into it to give it a white, smooth surface that would allow the ink to adhere to the skin without bleeding through.

traced a preexisting illustration. One technique for tracing, called pouncing, required the illuminator to prick the outline of the design with a pin hundreds of times. The outline was then placed over the vellum sheet to be illuminated and dabbed with charcoal dust to create a dotted line. This line was then covered with permanent black ink and filled in with colored ink.

Skilled illuminators, valued for their talents for creating unique designs, worked freehand. They first lightly cross-hatched the blank space that would receive the decoration with ink to create small squares of equal size. Using the cross-hatching as a guideline for accurate spacing, illuminators then outlined the design with pencil or charcoal.

Occasionally illuminators wished to highlight a small area such as a halo. The preferred technique was to apply gold leaf. When the gold caught the light, it stood out dramatically from the rest of the page. To ensure good adhesion of the very thin leaves to the parchment, all gold work was done prior to the application of any ink. The key was to apply good quality glue to the vellum, followed by the gold. Once the glue dried, the gold was burnished with a smooth spoonlike tool to add luster.

A section of an illuminated manuscript highlights the artist's painstaking attention to detail in his depiction of Jesus and his followers.

Just as illuminated manuscripts represented the pinnacle of medieval manuscript production, the Book of Hours represented the pinnacle of all illuminated manuscripts. More copies of this type of prayer book were written than any other, making it the best seller of its time.

The Book of Hours

The medieval Book of Hours, as the name suggests, was a collection of prayers for each hour of the day. It was designed to assist people during times of private prayer. It also included other supplementary texts, calendars, and psalms for a host of holy days. The front section of all Books of Hours consisted of a calendar. Each of the twelve months had a full-page illumination depicting either the primary religious event for that month or seasonal activity.

The illuminations in Books of Hours were miniature versions of stories that their owners saw portrayed in stained glass, frescoes, or mosaics in their churches. Illuminations had two principal functions. On a practical level, they acted as bookmarks at a time when pagination and indexes had not yet been introduced. Illuminations were placed at the beginning of each month's prayers to allow readers to locate them easily. Secondarily, illuminations provided graphic representations of the texts they accompanied. Illustrations of Christ's birth, baptism, and crucifixion were intended to stir the same emotions as the larger images readers viewed while attending Mass. In this regard, Books of Hours linked home and church, as Wieck notes: "The entire celestial court, God and his cosmos, could be held within the palms of one's hands and taken home. . . . Used at home, the Book of Hours transformed one's chamber into a chapel."[40]

The central text is the Hours of the Virgin, which includes psalm verses, hymns, prayers, and readings to be recited during the eight canonical hours of the day: matins (before dawn), lauds (daybreak), prime (6:00 A.M.), terce (9:00 A.M.), sext (noon), none (3:00 P.M.), vespers (sunset), and compline (evening). In addition, these manuscripts include a calendar of the major feast days and the tools needed to calculate the changing date of Easter, the most important feast day of the Christian calendar.

Books of Hours were often custom crafted by commercial illuminators for a specific patron. One of these illuminators, the French artist Jean Fouquet, regularly customized his works by depicting his patrons at prayer alongside the most venerated holy saints. Fouquet also added personal touches to illuminations, such as the mottoes of his patrons, even though they bore no relationship to biblical stories.

The artists most well known for their Books of Hours were the Limburg brothers. The three brothers spent most of their careers working for one patron, the Duke of Berry, brother to the French king. The one Book of Hours they illuminated for him, which is widely considered to be the quintessential masterpiece of manuscript illumination, was *Les Très Riches Heures du Duc de Berry*, meaning the Very Splendid Hours of the Duke of Berry.

Les Très Riches Heures du Duc de Berry

Les Très Riches Heures du Duc de Berry set the standard for Gothic illuminations at the beginning of the fifteenth century and was the example followed by illuminators for the remainder of the Middle Ages. The book's fame derives from twelve full-page illuminations, one for each month, all of which contain remarkable subject matter, composition, color,

The Limburg Brothers

The three Limburg brothers, Paul, Jean, and Hermann, were from the city of Nijmegen in the Netherlands. Very little is known about them, but they are believed to have been born in the 1370s to an artistic family. Their father was a wood sculptor and their uncle worked as an illuminator for the French queen and for the Duke of Bourgogne. Paul is thought to have been the eldest and therefore the head of the workshop, but the first mention of any of the brothers in any medieval literature or correspondences was in the late 1390s when Jean and Hermann were apprenticed to a goldsmith in Paris.

In 1402, the Duke of Burgundy, Philip the Bold, paid the brothers to illuminate a Bible. In 1404 Philip died, and the brothers were forced to find another wealthy patron willing to hire them for illuminations. One year later, Jean, the Duke of Berry, hired them. The three brothers enjoyed a privileged lifestyle at the duke's many chateaux as his court moved from place to place in the course of a year.

In spite of the constant travel, the Limburg brothers completed several major Books of Hours, but only two remain in museums today—the *Très Belles Heures*, meaning the Very Beautiful Hours, housed at the Metropolitan Museum of Art in New York City, and the *Très Riches Heures*, which resides at the Musée Condé in Chantilly, France. The latter book was unfinished—although all of the major paintings were completed—when all three brothers died in 1416, presumably victims of the plague or some other epidemic.

and detailed realism. Each of the twelve illuminations is roughly the same size, 9 by 5.5 inches (23 by 14cm).

The Limburg brothers, departing from designs created for illuminations in earlier Books of Hours, shunned religious scenes in favor of depictions of everyday life in French cities and country villages. The illumination for each month showed a typical scene for that time of year, such as plowing fields, sowing seeds, hunting wild boar, harvesting crops, slaughtering livestock, and winter feasting. Within each illumination the brothers painted a mix of activities representing the privileged lives of the aristocracy interspersed with the suffering of the peasant class. In the illumination for the month of October, for example, the background is the imposing Palais du Louvre, the king's grand castle in Paris. In the foreground a peasant

A page from the illuminated Les Très Riches Heures du Duc de Berry *depicts French peasants sowing seeds in fields surrounding the Louvre palace in Paris.*

astride a horse plows a field while another peasant on foot casts seeds into the furrows.

The scene depicted in this illumination, as in the other eleven, is remarkable for the period. The extremely fine detail, which was a characteristic feature of the Limburgs' work, required delicate brushes and magnifying glasses. The sunny day, for example, casts shadows next to workers in the field, the man sowing seeds leaves footprints behind him in the freshly tilled soil, birds peck at the exposed seeds, and a peasant wearing tattered clothing looks toward viewers with a noticeable frown on his face. It is the opinion of H.W. Janson that, "The figures are meant to arouse our compassions for the miserable lot of the peasantry in contrast to the life of the aristocracy symbolized by the castle."[41]

The colors are another remarkable quality of the Limburg brothers' illuminations. The standard blues, greens, reds, and yellows are everywhere present, but in a variety of shades never before seen in Books of Hours. The blues of a sky or greens of a field vary as they do in nature rather than being the same throughout the illumination. The brilliance of the colors is equally stunning. This intensity

In the thirteenth century, Italian monk Guido d'Arezzo developed musical notation, which allowed monks to sing chants exactly as they had been composed.

is due in part to high-quality inks and to the innovative addition of glass ground to a fine powdery dust that reflects light and accentuates color.

Richly painted books that were created for storytelling represented a large part of medieval bookmaking but not all of it. Other written materials were produced when the Church pioneered the process of notating music for the Mass on vellum.

Musical Notation

Music was an integral part of the Mass during the Middle Ages. Monks, priests, and congregations alike sang prayers. During the early period of the Church, singing was known as plainchant, today commonly called Gregorian chant because it developed during the sixth-century reign of Pope Gregory I. In the several centuries that followed, thousands of chants were created and sung, all from memory because musical notation had not yet been developed.

Not until the thirteenth century did the monk Guido d'Arezzo create a system of musical notation. He invented the four-line staff, which later evolved into the five-line system in use today. Using the four-line staff drawn with ink on vellum, Guido made marks that told singers whether to sing notes high or low and how long each should be held. Gradually Guido added other information to the four-line staff, indicating parts to be repeated, notes to be sung softly or loudly, and changes to timing.

The importance of this work is immense. Before the four-line staff and notation, every singer had to memorize the entire chant, often a new one every Sunday. Because many singers introduced deviations when teaching the chants to the next generation of singers, chants changed as time went by because no two singers learned them precisely the same way. Notation finally ended that problem because writing chants down ensured that all singers could sing them the same way, preserving them for later generations.

Those generations, however, profited from far more than simply the creativity of medieval composers during the latter part of the Middle Ages. Art historians are in general agreement that medieval art evolved over time and that each half of the period was a fair reflection of the culture in which it was created. Initially somber and restrained during the early centuries of chaos and conflict, it gradually came to express greater optimism about the worth of humankind and the beneficence of God. The debt owed to thousands of anonymous artists who kept art alive and vibrant for a thousand difficult years was especially understood by those who followed, the artists of the Renaissance.

The Renaissance produced giants such as Leonardo da Vinci, Michelangelo, Giotto, Brunelleschi, and Raphael, all of whom could not have produced their masterpieces had it not been for the pioneering work of the artisans who came before them. Had the skills of medieval artisans not elevated the primitive art of the early Middle Ages to the more colorful, realistic, and sophisticated works typical of the later Middle Ages, it is unlikely that the Renaissance would have achieved the status it holds today as the greatest period of Western art.

Notes

Introduction: Art Inspired by Faith

1. Dante Alighieri, *The Diving Comedy*. Cambridge, MA: Harvard University Press, 1914, p. 231.
2. Quoted in Marjorie Rowling, *Life in Medieval Times*. New York: Perigee, 1968, p. 156.

Chapter 1: Thoughts Constructed in Stone

3. Emile Mâle, *Art and Artists of the Middle Ages*. Redding Ridge, CT: Black Swan, 1986, p. 13.
4. Mâle, *Art and Artists of the Middle Ages*, p. 83.
5. Quoted in C.H. Lawrence, *Medieval Monasticism*. London: Longman, 2001, p. 1.
6. Quoted in Peter Fergusson, *Architecture of Solitude*. Princeton, NJ: Princeton University Press, 1984, p. 101.
7. Quoted in Franklin Toker, "A Sourcebook for Introduction to the History of Western Art," University of Pittsburgh, 2001. http://vrcoll.fa.pitt.edu/ftoker/tokerfile/0010sb01-10.html.
8. Tim Dowley, *Introduction to the History of Christianity*. Minneapolis: Fortress, 1995, p. 297.
9. Anne Fremantle, *The Age of Faith*. New York: Time-Life, 1965, p. 124.
10. Quoted in Fremantle, *The Age of Faith*, p. 136.
11. Gerald L. Browning, "The Spirit of Illuminated Color," *Angelus*, December 2003, p. 23.

Chapter 2: Sculpted Sermons

12. Mâle, *Art and Artists of the Middle Ages*, p 144.
13. H.W. Janson and Anthony F. Janson, *History of Art for Young People*. New York: Abrams, 1992, p. 152.
14. Mâle, *Art and Artists of the Middle Ages*, p. 8.
15. Mâle, *Art and Artists of the Middle Ages*, p. 13.
16. H.W. Van Os, *The Art of Devotion in the Late Middle Ages in Europe*. Princeton, NJ: Princeton University Press, 1995, p. 104.
17. Jan Mainzer, "Arts and Values," Marist College, 2002. www.academic.marist.edu/mainzer/notes15/avn15.htm.

Chapter 3: Painted Icons

18. Leslie Ross, *Artists of the Middle Ages*. Westport, CT: Greenwood, 2003, p. 123.

19. Ross, *Artists of the Middle Ages*, p. 125.
20. Quoted in Konrad Onasch and Annemarie Schnieper, *Icons: The Fascination and Reality.* New York: Riverside, 1997, p. 233.
21. Cennino Cennini, *The Craftsman's Handbook.* New Haven, CT: Yale University Press, 1933, p. 27.
22. Onasch and Schnieper, *Icons*, p. 161.
23. Quoted in Beyond Books, "Early Medieval Painting," 2005. www.beyond books.com/art11/2e.asp.
24. Janson and Janson, *History of Art for Young People*, p. 122.
25. Alphonse Didron, *Christian Iconography: The History of Christian Art in the Middle Ages.* New York: Frederick Unger, 1968, p. 194.
26. Quoted in Onasch and Schnieper, *Icons*, p. 263.

Chapter 4: Biblical Stories in Tile and Glass

27. Quoted in Toker, "A Sourcebook for Introduction to the History of Western Art."
28. In Italy Online, "Guide to the Byzantine Treasures," 2004. www.initaly. com/regions/byzant/byzant4.htm# santclas.
29. Friedrich Heer, *The Fires of Faith.* New York: Newsweek, 1970, p. 139.
30. Quoted in Georges Duby, *Medieval Art: Europe of the Cathedrals, 1140–1280.* Geneva, Switzerland: Skira Art, 1995, p. 105.

31. Janson and Janson, *History of Art for Young People*, p. 160.
32. Eldred Aelfwald, "Medieval Architecture: The Rose Window," Wittsend Library, 2002. http://dragon_azure. tripod.com/UoA/Med-Arch-Rose-Window.html.

Chapter 5: Art to Celebrate the Mass

33. Stephanie Brown, *Religious Paintings: Christ's Passion and the Crucifixion.* New York: Mayflower, 1979, p. 7.
34. Ellen Ross, *The Grief of God.* Oxford, England: Oxford University Press, 1997, p. vii.
35. Quoted in Paul Halsall, "An Inventory of Church of Staffelsee, 812," Fordham University, 1998. www.ford ham.edu/halsall/source/812Staffsee. html.
36. Exodus 28: 3, 4.
37. Quoted in Duby, *Medieval Art*, p. 13.

Chapter 6: Painted Prayers

38. Roger S. Wieck, *Painted Prayers: The Book of Hours in Medieval and Renaissance Art.* New York: George Brazillier, 1997, p. 14.
39. Jean Décarreaux, *Monks and Civilization.* Garden City, NY: Doubleday, 1964, p. 336.
40. Wieck, *Painted Prayers*, p. 22.
41. Janson and Janson, *History of Art for Young People*, p. 260.

For Further Reading

Jean Décarreaux, *Monks and Civilization.* Garden City, NY: Doubleday, 1964. This work, aimed at the adolescent audience, explains the role that monks played in saving and preserving the art and culture handed down from the Greeks and Romans that might otherwise have been lost during the Middle Ages.

Tim Dowley, *Introduction to the History of Christianity.* Minneapolis: Fortress, 1995. This is an excellent book for the general reader. The author provides basic information about the history of Christianity that is well illustrated with many beautiful full-color photographs of religious art.

Anne Fremantle, *The Age of Faith.* New York: Time-Life, 1965. This book provides an excellent readable account of Europe during the Middle Ages. Its focus is on the development of the Christian Church and its influence. Included is an excellent collection of photographs and selection of medieval art.

Friedrich Heer, *The Fires of Faith.* New York: Newsweek, 1970. This book covers Christian art from the late-fourth-century Roman Empire to the fifteenth-century fall of Constantinople. The book is a good mix of commentary and reproductions—both black-and-white and color—of medieval art.

Maidie Hilmo, *Medieval Images, Icons, and Illustrated English Literary Texts.* Burlington, VT: Ashgate, 2004. This book provides a clear discussion of medieval icons and how they were later used in early English literature. The author provides insights and interpretations to many of the more commonly reproduced icons.

H.W. Janson and Anthony F. Janson, *History of Art for Young People.* New York: Abrams, 1992. Intended for the teenage audience, this book is a simplified, easily read version of H.W. Janson's better known work, *History of Art.* Janson explores art from the ancient world to the contemporary, mixing commentary with color art reproductions. One of the four major parts of the book is dedicated to art of the Middle Ages.

Justin Kroesen, *The Interior of the Medieval Village Church.* San Diego, CA: Thunder Bay, 2005. This work presents a photographic essay on dozens of medieval churches through northern Europe. Each essay describes in detail the architecture of one church that includes materials, size, decorations, and unique features.

Marjorie Rowling, *Life in Medieval Times.* New York: Perigee, 1968. This detail-packed book focuses on different classes in each chapter, including nobility, students, traders, monks, and artists. It is a good general overview of life in early and late medieval Europe, primarily France and Germany. The book is enhanced by drawings and photographs of medieval art.

H.W. Van Os, *The Art of Devotion in the Late Middle Ages in Europe.* Princeton, NJ: Princeton University Press, 1995. This book is well illustrated and basic enough to be read and understood by young audiences. The author covers two centuries of medieval art, highlighting the best-known and most important works of the times.

Works Consulted

Books

Dante Alighieri, *The Divine Comedy.* Cambridge, MA: Harvard University Press, 1914. Dante's work is a fanciful journey through hell, purgatory, and heaven. As he visits the three, the author speaks with people and makes social and political comments about their lives.

Stephanie Brown, *Religious Paintings: Christ's Passion and the Crucifixion.* New York: Mayflower, 1979. Brown presents a history of medieval paintings that depict the major moments in the life of Christ. The book contains a large number of high-quality full-page photographs with accompanying text explaining the significance of each work.

Cennino Cennini, *The Craftsman's Handbook.* New Haven, CT: Yale University Press, 1933. Cennini wrote this handbook as a primer for painters to instruct them in the practical arts of painting. His book covers hundreds of topics, including advice on selecting a master painter, making paints and paintbrushes, and painting frescoes.

Christopher De Hamel, *Medieval Craftsmen: Scribes and Illuminators.* Toronto, Canada: University of Toronto Press, 1992. This book provides an excellent history of the copying and illuminating of medieval texts as well as a variety of color photographs of unusual and beautiful manuscripts.

Alphonse Didron, *Christian Iconography: The History of Christian Art in the Middle Ages.* New York: Frederick Unger, 1968. This well-illustrated book focuses on a small number of symbols widely used in icon paintings. The meaning of each symbol is explored, as are their changes over the centuries.

Georges Duby, *Medieval Art: Europe of the Cathedrals, 1140–1280.* Geneva, Switzerland: Skira Art, 1995. The author provides a well-illustrated book detailing the evolving characteristics of Gothic cathedrals throughout Europe.

Peter Fergusson, *Architecture of Solitude.* Princeton, NJ: Princeton University Press, 1984. Fergusson provides a detailed account of early Christian architecture found in monasteries throughout Europe. The book includes architectural drawings and photographs that complement his commentary.

C.H. Lawrence, *Medieval Monasticism.* London: Longman, 2001. This book is a superb scholarly endeavor that is considered one of the best overviews of medieval monasticism. Lawrence is a senior scholar who presents a variety of descriptions and discussions of monks, their place in European history, and their intellectual environments.

Emile Mâle, *Art and Artists of the Middle Ages*. Redding Ridge, CT: Black Swan, 1986. This work demonstrates some of the finest scholarship and insights about what motivated medieval artists to practice their crafts and how they perfected them.

Konrad Onasch and Annemarie Schnieper, *Icons: The Fascination and Reality*. New York: Riverside, 1997. This large art book, filled with over five hundred high-quality color illustrations, documents the history of Byzantine icons. This book provides a broad overview of the pictorial themes of icons and includes information about painters, different types of icons, and printing techniques.

Ellen Ross, *The Grief of God*. Oxford, England: Oxford University Press, 1997. The author cites dozens of medieval literary sources and pictorial evidence to discuss the nature of medieval attitudes toward the suffering of Christ. She concludes that to the medieval mind, renderings of the wounded Jesus were statements of God's mercy and love.

Leslie Ross, *Artists of the Middle Ages*. Westport, CT: Greenwood, 2003. Ross examines the works and lives of several of the more famous and influential artists of the Middle Ages. Each account investigates aspects of the artists' lives, materials, methods, and patrons.

Whitney S. Stoddard, *Monastery and Cathedral in France*. Middletown, CT: Wesleyan University Press, 1966. Stoddard's book provides detailed accounts and numerous photographs of twenty churches and cathedrals across France. His discussion begins with sixth-century monasteries and concludes with the great thirteenth-century Gothic cathedrals.

Roger S. Wieck, *Painted Prayers: The Book of Hours in Medieval and Renaissance Art*. New York: George Brazillier, 1997. This beautiful art book was published to commemorate the Pierpont Morgan Library exhibition of illuminated manuscripts. It contains more than one hundred color plates from illuminated manuscripts with accompanying commentary.

Periodical

Gerald L. Browning, "The Spirit of Illuminated Color," *Angelus*, December 2003.

Internet Sources

Eldred Aelfwald, "Medieval Architecture: The Rose Window," Wittsend Library, 2002. http://dragon_azure.tripod.com/UoA/Med-Arch-Rose-Window.html.

Beyond Books, "Early Medieval Painting," 2005. www.beyondbooks.com/art11/2e.asp.

Jackie Craven, "The Church of St. Denis," About Architecture, 2005. http://architecture.about.com/library/blstdenis.htm.

Paul Halsall, "An Inventory of Church of Staffelsee, 812," Fordham University, 1998. www.fordham.edu/halsall/source/812Staffsee.html.

———, "Medieval Source Book: Abbot Suger: On What Was Done in His Administration," Fordham University, 1996. www.fordham.edu/halsall/source/sugar.html.

In Italy Online, "Guide to the Byzantine Treasures," 2004. www.initaly.com/regions/byzant/byzant4.htm#santclas.

Neil MacDonald, "A Historical Perspective—III," Olive Leaf, 2003. www.peace.mb.ca/06.Unity/xneil06.htm.

Jan Mainzer, "Arts and Values," Marist College, 2002. www.academic.marist.edu/mainzer/notes15/avn15.htm.

Erwin Panofsky, "Abbot Suger of Saint-Denis," Columbia University, 1999. www.columbia.edu/~eer1/suger.html.

Franklin Toker, "A Sourcebook for Introduction to the History of Western Art," University of Pittsburgh, 2001. http://vrcoll.fa.pitt.edu/ftoker/tokerfile/0010sb01-10.html.

Index

Picture Credits

Cover photo: The Bridgeman Art Library/Getty Images

Maury Aaseng, 17, 20, 23, 38 (map), 58

Alinari/Art Resource, NY, 48

© Paul Almasy/CORBIS, 31

© Archivo Iconografico S.A./CORBIS, 26, 27, 45, 49, 77, 79

© Arte & Immagini srl/CORBIS, 71, 86

© Bildarchiv Monheim GmbH/Alamy, 29

Camerphoto/Art Resource, NY, 73

© Elio Ciol/CORBIS, 38 (photo, center right), 57, 72

Corel Corporation, 22 (inset), 63 (left and bottom right)

© Danita Delimont/Alamy, 32

© Werner Forman/CORBIS, 38 (photo, top right)

© Eddie Gerald/Alamy, 38 (photo, bottom left)

Giraudon/Art Resource, NY, 21

© Rainer Hackenberg/zefa/CORBIS, 55

© Lindsay Hebberd/CORBIS, 38 (photo, bottom right)

© Andrea Jemolo/CORBIS, 41

© Mimmo Jodice/CORBIS, 54

© Jon Arnold Images/Alamy, 12

© David Lees/CORBIS, 68

Erich Lessing/Art Resource, NY, 52, 67

© Massimo Listri/CORBIS, 42

© Dennis Marsico/CORBIS, 16

© Courtesy of Museum of Capitular de la Catedral (Girona); Ramon Manent/ CORBIS, 82

© Adam Myk/Alamy, 61

PhotoDisc, 22

Photos.com, 60, 63 (top right)

© ReligiousStockOne/Alamy, 15

Réunion des Musée Nationaux/Art Resource, NY, 85

© Hans Georg Roth/CORBIS, 35

Scala, Art Resource, NY, 44, 65

© Geray Sweeney/CORBIS, 13

© Sandro Vannini/CORBIS, 9

© Adam Woolfitt/CORBIS, 19

About the Author

James Barter received his undergraduate degree in history and classics at the University of California in Berkeley, followed by his graduate degree in ancient history and archaeology at the University of Pennsylvania. Mr. Barter has taught history as well as Latin and Greek.

A Fulbright scholar at the American Academy in Rome, Mr. Barter worked on archaeological sites in and around the city as well as Etruscan sites north of Rome and Roman sites in the Naples area. Mr. Barter also has worked and traveled extensively in Greece.

Mr. Barter resides in Rancho Santa Fe, California, and lectures throughout the San Diego area.